THE LAST
PILGRIMAGE

THE LAST

PILGRIMAGE

MY MOTHER'S LIFE *and*

OUR JOURNEY

to SAYING GOODBYE

LINDA DALY

| COUNTERPOINT | BERKELEY, CALIFORNIA |

Library of Congress Cataloging-in-Publication Data

Daly, Linda, 1966-
The last pilgrimage : my mother's life and our journey to saying goodbye / Linda Daly.

pages cm
ISBN 978-1-61902-117-4 (hardback)
1. Daly, Nancy, 1941-2009. 2. Pancreas—Cancer—Patients—Family relationships—United States. 3. Mothers and daughters. 4. Daly, Linda, 1966- 5. Philanthropists—United States—Biography. 6. Death—Psychological aspects. I. Title.

RC280.P25D353 2013
616.99ʾ4370092—dc23
[B]

2013001212

ISBN: 978-1-61902-319-2

Cover design by Ann Weinstock
Interior design by Elyse Strongin, Neuwirth & Associates

Counterpoint Press
2560 Ninth Street, Suite 318
Berkeley, CA 94710
www.counterpointpress.com

Printed in the United States of America

LEO AND JULIANNA
you are my two greatest blessings

Brian's desperation shattered the calm as he clawed his way back up to the driver's seat of the RV.

Go Go GO!

Bobby looked to his right, miraculously knowing exactly how to react. Our thirty-foot Sundowner finally performed as we needed it to, just as the maroon Cutlass Supreme began circling us. Its windows were blacked out, but the passenger side window, rolled halfway down, revealed a male figure grinning at us maniacally, as if we were his dinner. I had seen the vehicle approaching us from the driver's side, hoping they were only late-night shoppers looking for a spot in the lot. I checked the time; it was well past 10:00 PM on that Friday night. We were lost.

After only two days on the road, attempting to get my mother back home to her bed in Los Angeles, we had simply exited the highway outside of St. Louis looking for a place to stop for the night. The logistics of this trip, until this point, had been fairly smooth. But this time, even the full moon couldn't light our way. I remembered someone imploring us to keep the Arch to one side of us, but I couldn't remember which side, or why that was even important.

We knew we were in a bad neighborhood, having seen the burned-out buildings and abandoned cars as we drove through. But we had to stop. She was dying. Something inside told the three of us—my two brothers and me—that this was it. Conflicting emotions began to get the better of us: Sadness, exhaustion, and a twinge of relief combined to keep all of us on edge. Idling in a well-lit Home Depot parking lot seemed as safe a place as any to contemplate our situation.

Oh, how wrong I was.

Our eyes were wide, bodies almost frozen in fear. Now another car arrived and sped in behind us. We were blocked in. The two cars circled, slowly at first, sizing up their bounty, so obvious we must have seemed in our bulky RV and lack of direction. I had never felt physically threatened before, but maybe my brothers had, since their reactions were lightning fast. I sat there, frozen and numb, incapable of doing anything.

Panic set in as Bobby put the pedal to the metal and we burned rubber out of there. Plates, food, mugs of freshly made coffee, and the last bit of cream skidded off the counter and all over the floor.

The menacing cars circled around again, trying to cut us off, but Bobby made a dash for the exit. He swerved to the right and made a deft escape to the empty and dark road. Brian magically appeared in the passenger seat to navigate our way to the nearest highway on-ramp. The two cars were still in pursuit, even with all of Bobby's Indy 500 moves. I only hoped Mom hadn't rolled off the bed.

Keep breathing, I reminded myself, even as chaos exploded inside the RV. One step at a time, we will get out of this. One breath at a time, we will find the highway. One step at a time, we will live to tell this story.

We all checked the rearview mirrors, watching the cars stop short of following us onto the highway. I guess we weren't worth that sort of chase, after all.

Finally, the sound of my own breathing had calmed me down. I began to feel the inner peace I had so desperately wanted and needed. A thousand feathers brushed my skin. Laurie, my mom's nurse, who surely regretted volunteering to drive home with us, crawled out from the back of the RV. Her two simple words: *She's gone.*

My mother was dead. God was close. My heartbeat was all I heard.

I.

MIRACLES

| CHAPTER ONE |

In 2006, my mother, Nancy Daly, was at the top of her game. Los Angeles's former First Lady from 1993 to 2001 was now the board chair at the Los Angeles County Museum of Art. She was overhauling its board of directors by bringing in younger patrons who were invested in the future of Los Angeles. She had founded two important local children's charities that continued to improve with age. She served on numerous advisory boards across the city and country. Her career as a child advocate had branched out by shaping legislation to help abused children and programs to help keep families together. In the process, she had become the go-to person for issues with L.A. County's rugged bureaucratic landscape. She was a role model for those wanting to be in that world, and one for women who just wanted to be as strong and feminine as she was. She was a beautiful, happy, selfless, and extremely well dressed woman, busy doing exciting things, and had healthy, thriving children and grandchildren. She was on an incredible trajectory that was only getting more exciting as the days moved on.

So, of course, that was when things went wrong.

After returning from extensive overseas travel in May, my mother was feeling very ill. It was initially thought to be a bad stomach bug, attributed to something she had picked up while traveling through India on an art tour or maybe when she joined me in Rwanda for a humanitarian trip that eventually took us to the Kibera slum of Nairobi and hilltop visits to AIDS victims on Lake Victoria. While in the hotel in Kigali, Rwanda, she had complained her stomach was terrible. It groaned and gurgled and made her feel nauseous. She had a sour taste in her mouth and chronic diarrhea. No matter what she ate, it shot straight through her. She said it felt like her body had stopped digesting food, which, in turn, sent her to the bathroom as soon as she finished eating. Knowing she had been on malaria medicine, we thought it could have been just a nasty side effect. But since we had a week left in Africa, she decided to continue the malaria medicine and just doubled up on her Pepto and Imodium to make it through the rest of the trip.

A week after returning home, I called to see how she was feeling. My mom confessed to me that she still felt queasy, even though she had stopped her malaria medication upon return. Regardless, she didn't discuss any further action with my brothers and me, except to tell us that she had paid a visit to her internist of many years, but he was hesitant to label it anything more than an adverse reaction to her malaria medication, like we thought. His course of treatment was to wait and see if it resolved itself. In the end, however, it was her girlfriends who prevailed upon her, insisting that she have an ultrasound just to make sure it wasn't anything serious. She told me she was going, which I agreed was the smart thing to do. Silly me was still wondering which protozoa had invaded her intestines.

I was sitting at the desk at my dad's ranch in Calabasas, where I worked overseeing the care of all the animals and the vegetable gardens, when I got the call that her ultrasound revealed two spots on either end of her pancreas. I was scheduled to go to Jazz Fest in New Orleans with my childhood friend Haydn that weekend, but this call changed everything. Cancelling the trip was my first thought, and then working on how not to have a full-blown panic attack was the next. In quintessential Nancy style, she told me I should still go and have fun. It will be a good distraction for you, she said, since there was nothing really concrete to do at that moment.

But that was the difference between my mother and me. She kept to her schedule regardless of how big the crater in the road. I, on the other hand, picked my cuticles, ate too much, and worried. For me, nothing was more satisfying than playing out every what-if circumstance with some red wine and potato chips. That way, I would have all my bases covered if any of them came to fruition.

At times I was envious of her brilliant coping strategy. But I didn't want to take the trip because I wanted to be as close to her as possible, crawl in bed with her, keep her from her appointments so I could be a scared little girl and she could comfort me. Ironic, too, because that wasn't the kind of mother she was. When I was sick, which was often when I was young, she tended to me, but once she determined my time at home eating tea and toast was over, I had to suck it up and go back to school.

Part of me still felt like that little girl. My mom remained my idol. I adored her and felt lucky to be her daughter. I relished every moment with her and lived vicariously through the morning-after stories about her parties, the famous people she knew well, and the intimate details of some socialites' lives while I was at home in baggy sweats and no makeup. My life was far simpler than my mother's, and that made me happy. I didn't want it to be any different.

Hearing of an unidentifiable health crisis was sending me to a dark and scary place I had not been since I was a child. Our parents are the ones who are supposed to take care of us. They are supposed to be our constant, not fall ill with unspeakable diseases that threaten their roles in our lives. I was so afraid of the emotions and what-ifs that were zooming through my brain with increasing speed. I still defined myself as Nancy's daughter. Who would I be if she were gone? The fear of losing my anchor was beginning to overwhelm me within the few moments since I had learned of her faulty pancreas. I was always hesitant to let my mom know how much I depended on her, since I was afraid my emotional security would be taken away from me. What if this was really bad?

My vision started to narrow and darkness crept into my peripheral vision. My blood rushed to the surface of my skin and I thought I might faint. My scalp was tingly, just moments before a panic attack. I knew this pancreas situation was just going to get worse. I wanted to be in a magical bubble with her where I could stop time and keep her safe. Wishful thinking, but then again, my mom lived in that world where if you wished something away, it just might disappear. She was the queen of pretending nothing was wrong. But this time her voice was distant and sad. She knew more than she was telling me, but I wasn't going to press it because, really, I didn't want to know any more. Time would unfold the whole truth soon enough. I knew one thing about the pancreas: It was not something one could shrug off if it didn't work well. Without it, a life of diabetes would follow, and that was the best-case scenario. But "two spots" in my mind meant only one thing: cancer. She had already had a close friend who had died of this incurable disease. With him, the cancer had gone into remission once, then came back with a vengeance, eventually spreading everywhere.

If I could just slow my breathing, I would be all right.

Usually I preferred to cut to the chase. If bad news is to be shared, just lay it on me and I will deal with it as I do, quietly and introspectively, with the goal of figuring out how to make it better. That sounded great in theory, but I was far too afraid to initiate that conversation. Usually, my way of coping kept me out of my mother's land of wishful thinking. But this time living in the limbo of worrying about what I could not control was more attractive than knowing the severity of the situation. Since she was not one to dwell on anything, and hated entertaining the negative, there was no use discussing my fears with her anyhow. I knew from her tone that if I showed anything less than absolute strength, she would stop telling me what was happening. I was never sure, though, if it was for my sake or for hers.

For my mother, uttering that c-word was not yet applicable. She never worried herself over the future; she just remained busy until things were answered. She worked everything into her schedule, no matter what it was. This illness was going to have to fit in between her other engagements. She made time for everyone, rarely turned down an invitation, and hardly ever had down time. Even vacations were packed with activity.

I was hoping she would take the opportunity to slow down now, since her life may be on the line. Perhaps a little reflection on how to do things differently, a little less candy and Diet Coke and maybe a quieter life. I wanted her to stop activity and work with me on preserving her life, since I was already in that worst-case scenario. I wanted to be her problem solver. But she was not someone anyone could take care of. She was going to approach this her way and her way only. My mother always did things exactly the way she wanted.

At the close of our conversation, my mother asked that I inform my dad, from whom she had been divorced since the early 1990s, since he was flying his pigeons at the ranch that day. Although my dad had run Warner Brothers with Terry Semel for twenty years and then ran the Los Angeles Dodgers, he had been an avid pigeon collector since his boyhood days in Brooklyn. He always wanted a space big enough to fly as many birds as he wanted, so voilà, the ranch. Since there was plenty of room, the horses, chickens, goats, sheep, donkeys, ducks, and miniature pigs that I oversaw filled the space with personality and noise. Always one to do what was asked, I said yes to my mom, even though being waterboarded sounded more appealing than the pending conversation with my dad.

I hung up the phone and sat for what seemed like an eternity. My hands were on the desk, palms down, and I could feel the moisture build up between them and the desk. My feet were square on the floor, like I was going to push back the chair at any second, but I couldn't move. I could feel the sweat start to drip through my pink T-shirt. My breaths were being counted one through five on the inhale, six through ten on the exhale— a handy skill I had learned to combat a panic attack. I could hear nothing else. A fly landed on my pinky and I came back to where I was, and the soundtrack of my work brought me back to reality. The goats, sheep, and donkeys were singing in unison as their feed was being placed in front of them. I could also hear my father's footsteps on the gravel outside the barn, so I finally stood up. I don't know what was propelling me towards him, since I have no memory of getting there. It was a moment where I knew I was speaking but wasn't aware of the words coming out of my mouth. I simply blurted out that there was something wrong with Mom.

My father and I had not been known to talk about anything in depth. We were as close as we could be, without ever really talking about it. I knew I was loved, but was rarely told. Perhaps he was as afraid as I was that the exposure of our true feelings would somehow damage the relationship. Neither one of us would ever take that risk. Telling him about my mother would mean that I would be breaking our "keep it light" code of simple check-in calls to find out if everything was as it should be. I had tested our code once, my freshman year of college when a high school friend had died in a fiery car crash. He didn't know what to say to make me feel better, and so I learned not to tell him about my sadness. Besides, I had my mother for the emotional stuff. Disclosing this information about her meant I would have to expose a vulnerability and run the risk of seeing him emotional, and I wasn't prepared. I saw him cry only once, when my parents split up and, for the first time in our lives, we were leaving on a family vacation without him. I didn't want our dynamic to change, but it was going to have to.

Walking quickly out of the barn, I called after him. He turned with a smile. What else could I have needed except to talk about what summer vegetables we would be planting? He must have seen the weight in my face, because he stopped and faced me. As the words came out, describing my phone call with my mother, he shrank away from me. He clutched his heart as that same expression of deep sadness the day we left him for vacation clouded his face.

I watched his unshakable grief that wouldn't really go away until my mom returned from her surgery. All he said was, "Oh, my God. This is terrible, terrible news."

We didn't hug or look at each other again, because surely tears would follow and my dad wasn't someone I cried with.

Before my mom traveled to Africa, my parents had gotten together for lunch to mend fences and breathe a big collective sigh of relief that their three children had become successful happy adults and they had some wonderful, funny grandkids as well. As far as they were concerned, the future was a bright, happy place. Both of them were now married to spouses who were complete opposites of each other: my mom to Dick Riordan, former mayor of Los Angeles, who was gregarious yet absentminded where my dad had been understated and completely in control. My dad was married to Carole Bayer Sager, a songwriter whose music helped define a decade. (Needless to say, family dinners were never dull.) Carole was so talented that she was still discovering the levels of her skill and was always on a quest for deeper spirituality. The first thing we recognized was how much in love the two of them were. That wasn't something anyone could say about my parents when they were together.

I had a strong feeling things were going to change as I ended my day at the ranch. All of us would be talking about this insurmountable learning curve that we would reluctantly find ourselves on. That would bring on its own set of problems. Like a game of telephone, I would have to figure out what the interpretation of the facts was and what was really going on. Then of course there would be the question of why someone wasn't the first to find out the latest detail, something common to families with many interested parties. My mom's life of resisting care from anyone would be completely changed with all of us throwing in our opinions, and we certainly would have no problem voicing them now. We would be in her business and insist, as a family, on helping her out in any way we could. In my romanticized version of the future, we would band together and my mom would depend on all of us to help her through this crisis. It would forge our family together, and we would set an example for others on how to deal with what lay ahead. Emails would tie us together, and we would grow closer as we fought triumphantly against my mother's illness. Our former, carefully carved dynamic of speaking around the one in need, so not to upset them, would be forever changed.

One thing occurred to me as I made the left from Malibu Canyon onto the Pacific Coast Highway. With her health in question, I was going to have to come out of the shadows and start acting more like my mom, who always made everything look effortless and beautiful. I was going to have to do what my mother was doing, and that was to fit what might be something serious into my life without having it take over. All the years of watching her would be put to use, since my actions were going to be noted by others on a larger scale now. I was going to have to prove how strong I was.

After some serious consultations with local experts on the pancreas, it was recommended that Nancy have a Whipple procedure. This would remove the head of her pancreas, part of a bile duct, her gall bladder, and her duodenum. The only person in my mom's opinion to perform this operation was Dr. John Cameron at Johns Hopkins. At the time, he had done more of these than anyone else in the country.

The preparations for her trip to Baltimore were handled with little drama. Nancy's way was to calm everyone when they were at their most insecure by smiling and assuring them that our current predicament was not as bad as they were projecting. We labeled this her "Barbie mode." While some may think this was one of my mother's greatest strengths, we often thought it was one of her greatest weaknesses. When things got uncomfortable for my mother, she never let anyone see. Instead, she held her head high and put on a big smile and moved forward. It got her through everything. No one ever saw her flinch. We made fun of it because the more uneasy she became, the bigger the smile. Usually this happened when she was with Dick and he would do something embarrassing like leave food on his face while talking to some Nobel Prize winner. She just smiled, wiped his chin, and kept the conversation going.

She could juggle everything, be available for everyone, and still have time for her family. We used to joke that she could make a U-turn on Sunset Boulevard in her Chanel suit and Manolos while convincing the President of the United States to sign something in favor of underprivileged children as she fixed her lipstick in the rearview mirror. She was the ultimate graceful multitasker. It was enviable, but we would have preferred if she slowed down to enjoy the moment a bit more. I had become introspective and transparent in my emotions in reaction to her always making everything look so shiny and perfect on the outside. I complained about things, was far from perfect, and was often too blunt. I didn't sugarcoat anything, which probably made me look brash, but for all my mother's need for appearances to be perfect, I could not care less. I was messy most of the time and didn't really care what anyone thought.

However, given the circumstances, I tried to put on my best Nancy face in public. Ultimately, though, I had to shelter myself from outsider reactions to the news, because people said the stupidest things. Someone actually said to me, "Well, at least you had that trip to Africa together." I responded, "She's not dead yet," and walked away. Never spoke to that idiot again.

My mom and I were just hitting a new and wonderful point in our relationship. This is not to say that we didn't get along before; we always did. But now, we were more open. We were developing into best friends and it felt fantastic. It was the ultimate confidence booster knowing my mom had my back. At the time of her diagnosis, she was deeply involved with my children, regularly picking them up from school for special "Nana time," which invariably involved an influx of treats forbidden in my house—sugar and fast food—followed by totally unnecessary retail acquisitions. This was her favorite role, and I was not going to be the one to stop her. She and I spoke every day about what was going on in each other's lives. We asked each other advice on girlfriends, philanthropic activity, talked a lot about her work at LACMA, the most stressful post she'd ever held, which was at the same time the most incredibly exhilarating. We talked frequently of partnering on some philanthropic endeavor, she from the policy level, me from the grassroots, where we were both the most comfortable. We believed we could make a big impact together. We were finally seeing each other for whom we had grown into. The traditional mother-daughter relationship had evolved into something so much better. My mom was the most amazing woman I had ever known, and the possibility of losing her was more than I could fathom.

Between the weeks of her diagnosis and her actual surgery, Nancy lived life as if it were normal, even though the visual signs of her decline were increasing by the day. She was not one to dwell on the negative aspects of potential death, so she continued with her schedule until she had to leave for Baltimore. She was honored by the *Los Angeles Business Journal*, had meetings for her various boards and a luncheon fundraiser for International Medical Corps, the organization with which we had traveled in Rwanda and Kenya. She squeezed everything into those few short weeks before she left, leaving nothing hanging or incomplete. She paid absolutely no attention to the fact that, because her digestion was compromised, she was losing weight rapidly. She was turning yellow from jaundice. Her coloring was so bad, it looked like she had been dipped in toxic chemicals. There was no amount of tanning cream that could mask the absurd color of her skin. Coordinating her outfits and her signature round glasses to decrease the yellow of her eyes and skin was a challenge. I sat in her closet the morning of the International Medical Corps luncheon as we went through outfits to offset the jaundice. The blue cardigan made her look green, the brown suit made her look neon yellow, and the pink floral just made her look downright alien. At last, there was something concrete I could do to help. Given an actual task to complete made me feel slightly ahead of what was taking over my mother. Regardless of her shrinking frame and yellowing skin, she was still the beautiful mom I had always known. She was making lemonade out of lemons and employing me to do the same. For that I was grateful, especially since for these few weeks we were doing things together. I felt like together we would overcome whatever lay ahead. I was less afraid when I was with her. I was relieved she was not showing her feelings about her impending surgery. I don't think I could have handled it if I saw what was really going on inside her. I didn't ask how she felt and, for the first time, wanted to remain in her Barbie world, everything looking perfect.

Eventually, we settled on a long-sleeved grey turtleneck, since it was the only color that didn't clash with her skin, slightly puffy hair, and sunglasses. She looked very Madame X that day.

If she had any fear or jangled nerves, no one saw it.

The surgery for which she was scheduled was invasive, second only to a total liver replacement. In spite of her diet, which was crap—she ate pretty much whatever she wanted in small quantities so she could have dessert, and actually ate pie for breakfast—Nancy was in good physical shape. She worked out constantly and never gained weight. We hoped her physical condition would make recovery a bit easier, but there was just no telling what was really going on inside.

My mom's assistant Rita laid out the timeline for the East Coast trip in detailed itineraries for all of us. It was business as usual, another family trip with a more daunting destination. Only facts were discussed, not feelings, lest emotions get in the way of the task at hand. Family friends offered their plane, which meant my brothers, Bobby and Brian, Dick, my mom's best friend Joanne, and Tim, our family's longtime friend, could fly out with her. Because of a commitment at one of my children's schools, I was scheduled to take the red-eye to Baltimore later that night.

Lucky for me, another family friend offered to fly me on his plane to Baltimore. He claimed to have meetings in D.C. so would fly to BWI instead of Reagan National. (I found out later that he did not actually have any meetings; he wanted to fly me there because he thought it would make my mom happy.) En route, we discussed his marriage, which he admitted was not an easy one. He told me that when he had issues with his wife, he would call my mother, or have his wife call her. His question always was, "What would Nancy do?"

We talked about our children as well, what they liked doing, how entertaining they were, and how we could possibly love someone so much. But the topic that carried us the rest of the way to Baltimore was cancer. His father had passed away from it years before, and he had regret over what had not been said or done. He had stayed out of most of his father's health decisions because he thought it was the right thing to do, but in retrospect, he should have pushed his father for more treatment. Having just been initiated into the world of sick parents, I was not sure what I would do if that time ever came. I trusted my mom to do what was best for herself, but I questioned if her choice would actually be good for her children.

I wondered as the adult child, when does a parent's decision about her own care take precedence over what her child wants? And, does that decision make her selfish, or are we the grown kids the selfish ones? I wanted my mom to live for a very long time, so I was prepared to ask her to do whatever was presented to her so she would be around. At the same time, I was also torn. If I were the sick person, I don't know how long I would want to fight before the quality of my life began to suffer. How far would I go to make my kids happy?

I listened to my friend talk. He regretted not having pushed harder and urged me to push my mom to do what he hadn't done for his dad. As I took it all in, it became clear I was going to make sure my mom and I talked about everything. I didn't want to have any regrets, no matter the outcome. Already, this new territory was making me nervous.

When I got to Baltimore, I had enough time to throw my bags into my hotel room before taking a cab to the hospital. Everyone was already in Nancy's room, and their glassy eyes told me that we were all equally exhausted and petrified. But we didn't give in to outward signs of despair. Instead we emulated the highly scrutinized Barbie mode. My mom plastered a smile on her face, sat up straight, and with poise made it look like she was going in for some simple elective surgery. So smart, too, because her deflector shields made us all feel better. We kept up our part, chitchatting to keep things light. We did what we do best in a crisis: made each other laugh, did anything to distract from how close we all were to tears.

Our valiant camaraderie deserved a title, so "Team Nancy" was born. My brothers, Bobby and Brian, Dick, Joanne and John Agoglia, and Tim Green knighted ourselves as official members, helmed by Rita Brown, who was holding down the fort back in California. Having this new title brought us even closer together. We walked with Nancy from pre-op as far as the Johns Hopkins people would let us. She was pleasantly medicated, looked beautiful, of course, since she made sure she had gotten a mani/pedi and had her roots done prior to the trip. Knowing her, she got a wax as well, hoping that looking good on the outside was a reflection of the equal goodness inside.

We were told that it would be a few hours before they would come out to give us an update. We hunkered down in the uncomfortable, square upholstered chairs reminiscent of college libraries back in the '80s. Even though we were all trying to keep busy, most of us stared blankly out the window. After a short amount of time, one of the doctors, Dr. Ralph Rhuban, came out to deliver the bad news and the worse news. In addition to the Whipple procedure, my mother required the removal of her pancreas and spleen. Her pancreas had turned into a nonfunctioning fatty blob with cancer on either end. Dr. Cameron made the decision to remove everything surrounding her pancreas because he wanted to make sure the cancer hadn't spread. They acted quickly, not wanting to come out to ask if it were the right thing to do. Like we would have known how to make an educated decision anyhow.

As a result of this revised surgery, my mom was instantly diabetic and would have to take digestive enzymes with everything she ate, since all those physiological mechanisms were no longer available to her. Even with the removal of the surrounding organs, the cancer had spread outside its margins. It appeared that they had captured all the visible tumors, but the cells had made their move into the rest of her body. The first response to this was a chemo regimen once she recovered from the surgery. My brothers, Dick, and I asked many questions about what would be next. We all edged around wanting a label for this, but the doctors were not willing to give one to us.

After a little research, I discovered my mom had stage-four pancreatic cancer, and the life expectancy after diagnosis is approximately three to six months. The chances of her living more than five years after her diagnosis were roughly four percent.

Five years. Four percent.

I defiantly broke into Barbie mode upon reading this. This shroud of denial covered me like a heavy down comforter, would keep me wrapped in an insulated feathery dream world for as long as I needed. It also allowed me to shrug off the doctor's information like it didn't apply to us. My mother was far too extraordinary to simply be a part of the odds. It wasn't going to be like that no matter what anyone said. I was not willing to accept her demise within such a short period. Besides, Nancy Daly wasn't someone who would let something like this get the better of her. She would get the best treatment and beat the odds and there was no way about it. I spent no time thinking that she would die before the end of the year. We had too much to do together. I was firmly in my mom's fantasy world, shoved any reality aside, and continued to move forward. There would be no mourning yet; I simply did not have the time. Maybe I was more my mother's daughter than I was willing to admit.

By the time she woke, my mom was in a considerable amount of pain. She accepted the news as best she could but was only focused on recovering. I am not sure she understood how bad it was, because she never once said anything about the dire diagnosis. The only thing she happily shared was that the doctors fawned over the beauty of her liver, which was that of a much younger woman. One would have thought she had won the vital organ beauty contest.

Nancy was supposed to remain in recovery at Johns Hopkins for two weeks, and we had a hard time keeping her down. The day after surgery, she was convinced her life could resume the way it was before the diagnosis. Although healthy doses of morphine fueled this delusion, she wanted nothing more than to get out of the hospital and back to Los Angeles. Team Nancy had to confiscate her PalmPilot. She was inviting friends from all over the country to come hang out with her in the hospital and then forgetting she had spoken to them. As a result, I worked with Rita and became my mother's press secretary/director of communications. All correspondence went through Rita, then me. We hid my mom's phone and told her the battery had died and we lost the charger. She bought it for a few days but caught on once the dosage of pain meds was reduced.

It is not an understatement that the calls poured in. I calmed the nerves of former studio heads, listened to the most generous philanthropists cry, was asked by respected entrepreneurs if we needed a plane to fly us home. I listened to the greatest fears of some of the wealthiest people in Los Angeles and learned things I probably shouldn't have ever known, because in Los Angeles, my mother served many purposes to many people.

To some she was the strong-willed advocate for children. Some courted her for her influence with politicians and corporate giants. Others measured their own status as a reflection of how close they could be to her. Sounds so odd, but younger women climbing the social ladder vied to be on the short list for lunch with Nancy. I joked with my mom that she was L.A.'s own Miss Porter's, but really she was like the designer-clad godfather, without the mayhem and bloodshed. When there were disputes among her friends, she was the one they turned to in hopes of figuring things out. In one case, when two very close girlfriends had a historic falling out, my mother convinced everyone who knew the situation not to pass judgment or cut the offender out of their circles. One of them had established a well-known charity, and if the woman fell off the social radar, all the children that it helped would no longer receive services.

She put people to work, finding glimmers of goodness in some of the most difficult women in town. Friends and enemies would always gather together for the sake of my mom. It would be safe to say that the level of function on her numerous boards was due to her ability to get everyone to work together. And, if she met new people it meant an opportunity to find out how their passions to get involved in helping others could be realized. She was always able to see that person's best, pull the goodness out, and put it to good work.

Regardless of how someone fell into my mom's orbit, the outpouring of emotion and well wishes was a wonderful and honest example of how tragedy can bring people closer together. The extraordinary community around my mother had gone above and beyond on every level, and I was the first witness to everyone's love and commitment to her.

I did it all so my mother would recover in peace. I told everyone we'd be back in L.A. in two weeks and she would be up for visitors then. Even though people begged, seeing her in Baltimore was out of the question. She had to recover. I took a picture of my mom sitting on her bed a few days after the surgery, and she looked like she was in a low-budget motel, happy as can be. It looked like nothing bad had happened at all.

Even with my renewed sense of hope, there was a rising level of stress developing in the hospital room at Johns. Her relationship with Dick was becoming strained. My mom had been by his side as he recovered from both prostate cancer and open-heart surgery, so adding this to their plate was just too much. Neither one of them was a good patient; they both wanted to heal the way they thought they should. The threat of losing my mom may have been more than Dick could digest. He handled the whole ordeal poorly, was loud, interrupted a lot, and was just plain obnoxious. After a lifetime of being able to make things happen, Dick did not have the tools to fix this problem, so he acted out instead. His distress was causing more drama than my mom's recovery, and the snoring during his catnaps on the couch disturbed the people in the other room. It was enough to get all of us to join him in the bottle during daylight hours. A new task was added for those who remained in Baltimore: keeping Dick out of the room. So my mom could rest, we ran interference by taking him for walks, and out to lunch and dinner at the hotel.

As part of Operation Distract and Entertain the Former Mayor, my mother suggested that Dick and I partner up and make it our mission to find treatment for her when she returned to Los Angeles. So, while my mom was trying to sleep, Dick would be shouting on the phone. Maybe his loud voice would scare the rest of the cancer away, as the single malt came out earlier each day. He and I listened to what the Hopkins doctors had to say, researched established, new, and developing treatments around the country, and called every expert looking for a cure or the best and latest medical intervention that could possibly help.

For example, we were told that, contrary to established treatment, the traditional combination of chemo and radiation was not the best course of action after all. In fact, people were dying more rapidly with that combo, so we looked for the person in the country who had done the most innovative chemo regimes for pancreatic cancer. We booked travel to Arizona to see one doctor, talked to someone in San Francisco, a few in Los Angeles and at Johns Hopkins. It ate up time between fielding calls from the West Coast and gave us hope that even though pancreatic cancer felt like a death sentence, new studies were being done all the time. We thought we could get her into a trial, so we pushed for that once we got the same answers on which chemotherapies would be most appropriate.

While we were busying ourselves with problem solving, my mom followed the doctor's directions. She walked the halls, passed more gas than she ever thought imaginable, got the new insulin regimen down, and managed to make a truly miraculous recovery all with the aim of heading back to L.A. earlier than her doctor had imagined. Seeing this, I could feel the joy rising up through my body, putting a triumphant smile on my face. Maybe it wasn't denial that I clung to regarding my mother's situation. Her recovery confirmed my belief that there was more in store for my mother and maybe even for me. Could there really be a miracle at work? I wasn't certain, but I was going to live in it and relish it for as long as I was able. Nancy's time would come only when she was ready. I would bank on it.

When we finally boarded the plane to come home, we were armed with notebooks filled with phone numbers, email addresses, and ideas on what should happen next. My role of quiet daughter had officially changed. I was an active member of my mother's research team, dedicated to finding a cure for her cancer. I had joined the ranks of countless adult children who lived with hope that cancer would not take their parents. I listened to what anyone would tell me, commiserated with others who had lost their parents to this disease, and vowed I would not be one of them. We would be different. My mom would surely be in that four percent. I was going to do anything to make sure that was our truth.

So, with hope, a new life began in Los Angeles for the Daly family. Whatever was going on in our lives, cancer would play a part in everything we did. It was inescapable. The battle that lay ahead for me was twofold: to not let her cancer consume her, and to not let her cancer consume me.

| CHAPTER TWO |

The first few months of her recovery, coinciding with her sixty-fifth birthday, were spent with Dick in Malibu. My mother, who had never taken anything more than a vitamin, now had live-in nurses dispensing and monitoring more medication than I had ever seen. There were the digestive enzymes, a constant reassignment of insulin so her body could adjust to the new regimen, antibiotics, and anti-inflammatories. For her considerable and constant pain, she was given fentanyl lollipops to suck. She was supposed to rest but insisted on seeing all her friends whenever she wanted. I spent as much time with her as I could because I wanted to keep an eye on her.

Her tranquil, love-filled beach house had become the depressing House of Cancer, where I was soon uncertain of my place. This new environment reminded me of a recurring nightmare I had when I was a child: If I didn't make it back to my house before a certain time after school, all the houses on the street would change, and I wouldn't be able to find the right home. In the dream, I would knock on our front door, the door would open, and it would lead to a different interior with a different mom. I ran and knocked on all the doors on all the houses on our street, seeing all of those different interiors, until someone told me the rules had changed. At night the whole town changed, and I would have to wait until the morning to go back to find my house and family. It was always dark, always cold, and I never felt more alone. Was my mom looking for me? Did she even notice I was gone? While the beach house was always light and filled with the sound of the ocean, I never knew when I walked in the door if I would be in the sick house or the laughter house. I shivered every time I put my hand on the doorknob, holding my breath as I crossed the threshold.

Her initial recovery was not part of the fast track back to health, like my mom had planned. Early one morning, shortly after Nancy set up camp at the beach house, she was rushed to the hospital. Melida, the house manager, called me before 7:00 AM to tell me my mom was being transported by ambulance from Malibu to St. John's in Santa Monica. During all the excitement, Dick jumped into his own car while my mom was being put in the ambulance and managed to beat them to the hospital. I lived in Brentwood, about ten minutes from St. John's, and also arrived before the ambulance, so we stood in the ER waiting.

In came someone I had never seen. Beautiful Nancy was gone. In her place was a frightened woman, her face contorted by pain, fear, and anger. This stranger was sitting up, clutching the sides of the gurney, her knees bent with a sheet bunched up around her. What stood out most was the strain in her neck from how tightly she clenched her teeth. Her eyes were wild, searching for something she could not find. Dripping in sweat, she could not form words; nothing but grunts came out. She was experiencing acute agony in her abdomen and was petrified something had happened to the organs she had left. Maybe one of the sutures had ruptured and she was leaking internally. She looked at me with fearful eyes and said she was not sure if she could make it through this. If the pain was going to be like that, she didn't want any part of it.

I grabbed her hand and nodded. Grateful for my ability to be calm in emergency situations, I looked her in the eyes and started breathing deeply. I was hoping I could get her to breathe with me. I lowered my voice and told her she would be all right. The doctor would be there any moment, and we would get to the bottom of this. I was certain, I told her, that this was something *fixable*. I held her hand tightly as she started to calm down, forcing a little smile. I had never seen her in such duress before. If there had ever been any pain, I had never witnessed it. Until now.

The doctor explained the first action would be to relieve the pressure in her belly by inserting a tube down her nose. After that, they could assess the damage, if in fact there was any. Nancy had already been sedated but was still so hyped up that the doctor was hesitant to give her more. A tube was snaked down her nose as I squeezed her hand hoping if I hurt it she'd be distracted from what was happening. It was something Joanne did every time her kids got shots when they were little. They were always mad at her for hurting them, but they never felt the shot. Immediately, fluid gushed out through the tube. With that pressure relieved, it was astounding how quickly Nancy felt better.

She spent three days in the hospital, where they concluded her condition was not more cancer or complications from the surgery. It was a combination of her body adjusting to the removal of digestive organs and rebelling against the sudden attempt at healthy eating. While this diagnosis brought a huge sigh of relief, it turned out to be the first in a series of extremely distressing hospital visits for cancer- and surgery-related issues. Nancy began having quality-of-life conversations with us, all of which were premature, but we listened regardless. She was setting us up for what may lie ahead, but perhaps more, she was setting herself up in case her cancer really robbed her of what she wanted her life to be. None of us took her very seriously because she was far from what we knew was the end. From my perspective, she still had a very active life. She was premature in jumping back into her life, even though she was impatient with the amount of time it really took for her body to heal. Even though she was entertaining her demise, my mom looked healthy, had all her hair, and generally kept to her schedule, carrying her chemo bag inside her purse so she could still go to lunch.

I tried to be empathetic, but my permanent residency in La La Fantasyland prevented me from wanting to go any deeper. I convinced myself that her appearance was all that mattered. I had even decided to try to take on as much as I could so I wouldn't have to think about what cancer could ultimately do to her. I was becoming my mother in the ways I had never wanted. I was advising start-up charities on how to fund-raise and do outreach, had accepted a part-time job in develop-ment at International Medical Corps, was still working at my dad's ranch, and was running my own charity, in addition to parenting two children. I was exhausted, but with my mind occupied with other things, it seemed my plan for not dealing was working. I was too tired to think about anything other than what I had to do the following day.

I was talking to my mom one Friday on the way home from work, and she asked when I was going to come see her. I said I was so busy, I couldn't. She asked me why I was doing so much, and I started to cry.

I told her I was afraid to stop. I didn't know what would happen if I stopped and focused on her maybe not being alive for much longer. I finally choked out the sentence I had wanted to say since the first conversation at the ranch: "I am afraid you're going to die, and I can't deal with that."

She actually scolded me for acting like her. Clearly she knew that I was not meant to be her; I was meant to be me. She said that she was not going to die just yet; we had more things to do together. I should slow down and pay attention to what was happening, watch my children grow, and just spend time with her.

It was a relief to finally get those words out, and it was the beginning of letting my comforter of denial drop from around me. However, I was still not certain who I would be without her. The emotions I felt were just too frightening to discuss, but with the attempt at embracing that uncertainty, I went to the beach house that evening with the kids and spent the weekend.

Even though she looked good throughout the initial chemo process and was not as sick as we had thought she would be, the first six months were rough with hospital stays and extra doctor appointments. Nancy got through the worst of it, and life started to brighten. A year after the surgery, she had completed her chemo. Her tumor markers were finally within the normal range. She regained her health and dove into her former routine. Nancy had already outlived the prognosis for stage-four pancreatic cancer.

Life had virtually returned to normal for all of us, and I finally mellowed out. We fell back into a comfortable pattern as my mom resumed her life. She was working out again, traveling, even skiing. She was once again my champion. I knew she would beat this. I was relieved, felt justified in my secret claims that my mother would live a very long life and there was something greater at work. It was never something I discussed with anyone, because I didn't want to jinx it. But I was becoming a believer and couldn't have been happier.

♪

During this time, my mom developed an interest in marijuana as an alternative to the addictive fentanyl pops. Having known about the medicinal benefits of smoking marijuana, I prodded my mom to accept her girlfriend's offer of some primo weed. Within a few hours, a local dealer had dropped off an Altoids box filled with pre-rolled filtered joints. The dealer looked like a private-school mom. She was well manicured, carried a designer handbag, and drove a luxury car. Apparently the days of going through alleys in Hollywood for a dime bag were gone. This surreal landscape of illness and its accouterments, I was learning, was never what it seemed. It was confusing most of the time, but I learned quickly to roll with what was presented to me. The dealer, my mom's designer chemo bag, her newfound ability to inject herself with insulin through her stockings at a formal lunch—nothing was "normal" anymore. Fighting any of it was a waste of time, since everything changed so rapidly and without notice.

The dealer left her phone number with me, offered advice on how to properly smoke her product, which she claimed was powerful, and left. My mom was giggly at the prospect of getting high and didn't pay one bit of attention to what this woman had said. She insisted I join her, since she claimed not to have gotten high in years—already too much information for me. Clearly all boundaries were becoming blurred.

Unfortunately, she didn't quite grasp the idea of "just a hit," because she smoked one of those pre-rolled joints like it was a cigarette. As a result, my poor mom got so stoned she was out of commission for hours. That evening when she eventually woke up, she experienced one of pot's more delightful side effects: devouring whatever was in the kitchen. After the marijuana laws passed in California, she became a proud possessor of a medical marijuana card. As time went on she expanded her pot repertoire to include brownies, drinks, ice cream, and a fancy vaporizer, since smoking the joints hurt her throat.

Now that her pain was managed by a newfound love of the herb, she felt it was time to dig a bit deeper, since she had heard that cancer could recur without changes to her lifestyle. So, while discussing her health at her hair appointment, her hairdresser suggested my mom visit a woman named Vianna Stibal, who lived in Idaho Falls. According to the hairdresser, Vianna had an amazing energy that helped people heal from all kinds of things, emotional and physical. When my mom called to break the news of her discovery, I was grateful she was choosing to travel this road. I would have liked to go with her. I thought I could have used a little spiritual readjustment after the year we had survived, but really I just wanted to be the one to experience this with my mom. However, I was not invited.

Still, I was hoping she would come back armed with a new outlook that would slow her down a bit. Additionally, going to Idaho also meant getting away from Dick for a while. Things were still rather strained between the two of them, and they were apart more than they were together. She didn't discuss it much, but I know she was not happy in her marriage. She had hoped if she got better, so would the relationship, but it wasn't unfolding that way.

Next thing we knew, Nancy, accompanied by Tim Green, was on a plane to Idaho Falls to get rid of any emotional baggage that may have stood in the way of her healing. I did not speak to her while she was gone, and she was hesitant to give me details of what happened there when she returned. But after a little prodding, she told me she had attempted to come to terms with her childhood and her difficult relationship with her mother. She meditated a lot and stretched. She consumed a healthier diet. She was not a fan of the cuisine, though, and wanted to escape to the local 7-Eleven for candy, which messed up her insulin levels, but she didn't care. Whatever else she did up there, she came back a little lighter and more hopeful, enjoying the healing aspects of the experience. She brought home a necklace for me: a little rock on a leather cord. It had been blessed by Vianna and she said it would give me strength whenever I needed it. I immediately put it on and rubbed it between my thumb and forefinger, hoping for the strength I desired.

My mom was on her way to becoming an Oscar de la Renta–wearing Zen Master. She returned with helpful hints, crystals, and deep breathing exercises. She did not hesitate to share them with me when I was stressed or talked about negative things. However, all of this was comically ironic because while she was happy to dole out advice, she wasn't really walking the walk. Her terrible diet, her schedule, and her marriage were all things we thought should change if cancer was to really stay away. Instead, she worked all of her Zen Master moves into what already existed, happily extolling her knowledge on alternative and spiritual healing over a piece of cake and a glass of wine. I was happy to listen to her, though. I was hoping that the more she expounded on her newfound love of being peaceful, the more she would actually become just that.

The irony of her search for self-discovery for the whipped cream topping to her cancer-abatement sundae meant my mom had to become reflective—something she never had been. She didn't understand why anyone would dwell on the past when the

future had so much more to offer. It was the only way she knew
how to survive. She accomplished a lot with this attitude: For
her, things happened simply because she worked hard to make
them so. God had nothing to do with it. If she was going to get
better, it was up to her to find the right person to do that for her.

Other suggestions for permanent cancer removal came pouring
in as well. Stories of friends who knew someone who was healed
by crystals or herbs gave way to addresses and contact information or links to articles about what was happening across the
globe. Nancy never openly declined any of these suggestions.
Instead, we discussed the latest offering as if it were a decision
to be made about vacation travel. There were so many choices,
none in places any of us really wanted to go.

All of this added to the increasingly surreal and confusing
world of cancer. I was fairly certain I wanted my mom to just
be the healthy person she used to be, but I pretended to be
happy she was entertaining ideas for changing her life. I did
know, though, that none of this would stick, since she never
committed to anything for very long and was accepting these
suggestions to please her friends. As far as she was concerned,
she had beaten cancer. I was not convinced, since I knew she
had to make serious changes she wasn't interested in making.
Perhaps she knew she was on borrowed time and decided to
flip the bird to cancer and just live it up until her time came. It
would not have been the way I would have done it, but I was in
no position to throw in my two cents. When I did, I was pun-
ished. She stopped returning my calls. I wanted to be happy for
her, but I secretly wanted her to go to some detox colonic spa
where she would come back a vegan not addicted to sugar and

pain medicine. I wanted her to take her recovery seriously so she would be around forever.

It became harder to vocalize how I felt. I had a hard time trusting that our opinions were factored into her own health care decisions. I wanted to ask her, what about me? But I wouldn't dare. I didn't care that it may have been selfish and immature—she was my mom and I wanted her to think of me when she chose to eat candy and mess up her blood sugar, or anything else that would bring the cancer back and take her away from us. But she didn't want to be held accountable. She did what she wanted and told me after the fact. I wanted to honor her choices and trust that she would figure it out eventually, but I started to feel like I had a teenaged daughter who was hell bent on finding her own way through this without thinking of what the fallout would be. Instead, I ended up feeling mad, hurt, and left out.

While I was wrestling with my emotions and venting to my brothers, life went on. Every month, we waited breathlessly for the monthly call about her tumor markers. Eventually that became part of the routine, since one after the other proved she was just fine. The stress of those earlier days had eased up considerably. Cancer had become an undercurrent in our lives. Nothing was revolving around appointments, and my mother had graduated from a monthly scan to a three-month scan. Even that was pushed back to six months. She had returned to picking up my children after school for special Nana time. Her ways proved to be acceptable. Reluctantly, I let go some of my anxiety about her not taking her health more seriously. Really, I thought cancer had been beat.

Then there was the summer of 2008.

My mother went up to Sun Valley to spend some time with Joanne. She had become elusive about the details of her marriage, but we knew things were not right. My brothers and I had a sneaking suspicion she was up there cleaning out the house. While caught up in whatever she was doing, she ran out of one of her medications and decided it would not be a problem since they were coming home within a few days. She ignored the label on the bottle describing adverse side effects when stopped abruptly, thinking incorrectly this time that she would be the exception to the rule. We had no idea anything out of the ordinary was going on, except for the fact that she was not returning our calls. We figured she was out shopping.

Joanne's panicked call towards the end of their stay caught us completely unaware. She would not go into specifics, so we had to piece together what she was telling us and what my mom would disclose, which was only that she had "some side effects" from not taking her medication and was fine. We were furious with her for being so cavalier and secretive about her health. How dare she do this to us, since we thought we had gotten past all the juvenile behavior. Maybe she didn't want to worry us, but we found this act to be virtually unforgivable. It was clear she never really had any intention of fully informing us of anything anymore. It led to arguments and days of not speaking, since we took full advantage of the opening to blast her with everything we had been holding in since her first chemo.

Our supposed cancer-free paradise was sinking rapidly into a world of unknowns. Since when did my mom hide information from us? Whatever transpired up there, it must have scared her to the point where she was ready to make drastic changes. When she got back, she sent letters to each board, resigning immediately.

Another change upon return was that she and Dick had begun their unnecessarily messy divorce. It was unimaginable that the husband whose wife had stood by him through his own health crises was tossing her aside for another woman. She discovered this when she saw a wrapped gift on the floor of the car. She had a sneaking suspicion it was not for her, but asked anyhow, picking it up and thanking him for getting her a gift. As she began to unwrap it, he told her it was not for her but someone else. Needless to say, lawyers were called immediately, and the fight for their possessions began. So much for cutting out stress, since now she had to find a new house for herself.

Even though she was praised by those around her for finally taking care of herself, and was doing her best to remain healthy, cancer caught up with her. By late 2008, her tumor markers had risen; she went through terrible rounds of chemo that ruined her teeth, robbed her of her hair, gave her mouth sores, split her fingertips, and addled her brain. In her third year as a cancer patient, she began the downward slope. The real conversations about quality of life came up more often.

We were all on the scary and rapid descent into the depths of cancer. After what had become a routine PET scan, it was discovered the cancer had spread to the lining of her abdomen and into her lungs. Although this was no surprise, since she had been under an enormous amount of stress with the divorce, she downplayed the results. This time, we knew it was serious. There would be no casual remarks or actions from now on; we knew we would have to make our mom be straight with us. Her consolation to us was to have all of us join her at her next doctor's appointment. There, we could ask whatever we wanted. We were invited by my mom to be as honest as we wanted to be about statistics, side effects, and outcomes. She left it to us to decide what would happen next, and for this we were all relieved.

We were presented with a Hail Mary option, a trial chemo given to patients with advanced cancer. We were warned that this experimental regimen would be incredibly hard on her system, making all the other ones look like spa appointments. But if she could stick out the six weeks, it could bring her tumor marker levels down a bit—long enough to figure the next move, if there was going to be one. We understood this could do more harm than good given her incredibly fragile state.

Even knowing this, she was willing to do whatever she could to beat cancer. It sounded so daunting that we would have accepted her refusing the treatment. None of us liked the idea of our mom being used as a lab rat, but she wasn't close to giving up. She really thought any new option could be the cure she needed. She went forward with the chemo.

After her first treatment, I called her from a friend's house. She sounded pretty good but had to hang up abruptly because she became violently ill. Hanging up from her was one of the loneliest experiences I had ever had. There was nothing I could do to make the situation better. I cried to my friend, who had lost her father to cancer. I got the same hug and knowing look I would later give to others in my shoes, signaling that the end was closer than I was willing to admit.

I was living with the greatest sadness I had ever experienced, watching my mom deteriorate so quickly. In order to shield myself from the pain of losing her, I began to say goodbye to the mom I had my whole life and begin saying hello to this new sick mom. This sick mom was taking more pain medication than ever before, would often forget our conversations, and was lonely. She had been abandoned by her husband and was reticent to spend time with us, since she didn't want to be a burden. It was a terrible time. She slept more, ate less, and her quality of life declined rapidly. My son, Leo, was hesitant to spend time with her, since she was no longer the Nana he loved. My brothers and I spoke more often, as did my dad and Carole and I. We consoled each other and vowed to spend more time with her. I organized weekly dinners at her house, where I would cook. We would try to get my mom to laugh and think about good times, but she didn't want to eat much. The only food she could tolerate was ice cream.

None of this was easy. Her deterioration was devastating. I coped by eating as much as I could. Keeping life normal for my two kids was harder each day. I wanted to cry with my mom but wouldn't dare burden her with my encroaching grief. I was so utterly alone, scared, and desperately unhappy. Day after day we talked about her quality of life and how we were so proud of her for fighting. We wanted her to be OK to stop treatment. But she was not ready.

Throughout the time Nancy was on chemo, my brothers and I openly admired her for perseverance in this fight for her life. None of us thought we could do what she did. But it came to a point where we begged her to be honest about her expectations. She no longer had any quality of life. Bobby, Brian, and I were OK with whatever her decision would be and encouraged her to really think about it. At this point we were also going with her for her regular PET scans, disappointed each time with the cancer's advancement. Ultimately, after some difficult and emotional conversations, she found the courage to ask our permission to stop treatment. I can't even imagine how hard it was to do that, since she constantly worked to look her best when we were around. It was devastating to hear, but we knew her time was coming to an end. We told her how much we loved her, how brave and inspirational she had been. We were with her as much as possible and prayed her life wouldn't come to a close without all of us around her.

I had spent the entire time of my mother's illness preparing for this moment. All my worst-case scenarios had come to fruition. For as sad as I was, I thought I was as prepared as I could possibly be. I had stopped trying to do anything but remain present, since I didn't know how much time she had left. I moved out of Fantasyland when I was not with my mom but moved right back in whenever I saw her. I kept things light, didn't dwell on anything that would cause her stress. Everything was slowing down as we prepared for the emotional pain we knew would soon hit.

Even though Western medical intervention had given her much more time than had originally been thought, my goal-oriented mom decided to look elsewhere. For her, there was another world of available options. All her previous dabbling in the world of alternative cures was just practice for what the next few months would hold. All the recommendations we had gotten before were dusted off and invited in to conquer the House of Cancer. The time had arrived for her to fight from a different place now. Her fight was not yet over. She continued with a renewed fervor her exploration in alternative ways to cure her cancer and calm her soul.

The time had come for a real miracle.

CHAPTER THREE

Mom was raised in a very traditional Catholic home. So one might think, given the swift and painful progression of her cancer, she'd be hitting Lourdes and other Catholic sites historically known for miracle cures. But then you would be confusing her religion with her beliefs, which were not the same.

My mom had not been an active Catholic since I was in middle school. Her life as a participatory member of the religion had long before been soured by the Church, which she saw as inflexible, arcane, and dogmatic. When faced with her own mortality, she was not interested in praying for a cure. Nancy Daly wanted results, so the Catholic Church wasn't where she was inclined to start looking.

Her disassociation with the Church happened when she was attending Catholic school as a young girl. While careful never to be disrespectful, she challenged the doctrine fed to her by the nuns and priests. She thought that if God loved everyone, why were so many rules being laid down by people teaching His good word? She felt the nuns were restrictive. My mother was a free spirit, willing to test any limit, and really didn't think the nuns or priests had anything to do with the God they were representing. She was more interested in the latest fashions, sneaking cigarettes with her girlfriends, or hopping on the back of the motorcycle of the boy down the street. She was a rebel from the beginning, not caring to live up to the expectations of what a Catholic Girl in the 1950s was supposed to be.

When she married my father, the Church equally disillusioned them. They both questioned if they should raise their children in an atmosphere they felt had nothing to do with God. When Vatican II changed the rules in an attempt to modernize the Church, neither of them felt the need to follow what were clearly man-made decisions. For them, God didn't factor into now being able to eat meat on Fridays and no more Latin Masses. However, raising children outside the Church was really not an option for my parents. Being Catholic identified who they were, whether they liked it or not. Who would they be if they were no longer a part of that community? The extended family still went to church every Sunday, so rebelling in this sense may have been more frightening than just staying in it. They also felt it was important to raise their children with religion, so they made the choice to find a church in our neighborhood that suited our lifestyle. Back in the '70s, the Catholic Church was attempting to lighten up with more relaxed Masses, so the church we went to had a Folk Mass at eleven on Sundays. The young priest had more colorful robes than the old priest in our former church, who still spoke Latin. The liturgy was led by a sandal-wearing guitarist. There, my mother, in her wild prints and contemporary hairstyle, felt comfortable.

Years later, when she and Dick, a more traditional Catholic, decided to get married, they ran up against another religious dilemma. While having their ceremony conducted by a priest didn't really factor into their plans, they did have an offer from one who would, if they both would receive annulments. Getting annulments would declare their previous marriages had never existed. Regardless of why their divorces happened, neither my mom nor Dick would pretend the first marriages didn't exist. For the good and the bad, their previous marriages created children, careers, and extended networks of beloved family and friends. As far as my mother was concerned, if the sin of divorce meant she could no longer receive the sacraments in Mass, she was all right with that. Neither of them attended church regularly, so this would not become a deciding factor on whether or not they should get married again. Instead, they chose to be married by their friend, a federal judge on the U.S. Court of Appeals.

It was a storybook wedding at their home in Sun Valley, Idaho. It took place on the evening of Valentine's Day 1998. The snow was thick enough to blanket the yard, and it was cold enough for an ice rink to be poured on the driveway in front of the house so we could have an ice show and some skating. It was something out of a Currier & Ives print. My mom looked like she should be spinning on top of a cake, and Dick looked like someone straight out of *Doctor Zhivago*. Everyone—family, friends, and the community at large—was thrilled for them. We carried the images of that evening close to our hearts.

This joy was blemished a few months later when Cardinal Roger Mahoney of Los Angeles publicly announced that if

Los Angeles's First Couple set foot in his church, he would be compelled by Church doctrine not to give either of them the sacraments. In the eyes of the Church, not getting that annulment meant this marriage did not exist. My mother did not see any point to the Cardinal's tarnishing the fledgling marriage of Los Angeles's First Couple. They were happy, as were those around them. For my mom, the rules again had become too oppressive. She was an honest woman whose life was dedicated to helping others. If the arcane ritual of pretending your former marriage didn't exist was what was truly barring her from actively participating in a Mass, then she really didn't want to be a part of it.

Without the Church for clarity, my mom sought answers in less conventional ways. Around the time of my parents' divorce in the early 1990s, she spent a considerable amount of time with a woman named Darby, a spiritual therapist who lived in Santa Fe. My mom was determined to find an explanation for how she had reached that particular point in her life: divorced and seeking a depth of happiness and fulfillment she didn't realize she required. Darby believed the key to understanding oneself came from examining past lives and how they influenced who you currently were.

From Darby my mom also learned that when people become hurtful, those actions most likely stem from unresolved experiences in the past rather than from the simple act of wanting to inflict harm. Understanding this led to a sense of forgiveness and freedom my mother truly enjoyed. For instance, my grandmother never fully appreciated the force of nature that was my mother. My grandmother was solemn, controlling, and willing to withhold love from my mother when she did something my grandmother deemed unacceptable. While it would have been easy for my mom to carry that negativity and become the wallflower my grandmother preferred, through Darby, my mom traced her mother's life back to before my mom was born—back to when pictures of her mother showed someone with joy in her eyes. Between the births of my uncle and my mother, my grandmother was pregnant with a baby who died in her womb and had to carry that little girl to term. The birth of my mother, which should have been an incredibly joyous occasion, was a constant and painful reminder of what had been lost. My mother could never live up to the imagined perfect life of the one who had died before her, and she became the subject of angry words in failed attempts to break my mother's spirit. She was extremely fortunate, though, to have a loving father who showered her with more love and admiration than my mother could ever need.

As a result, this new understanding allowed my mom to understand her mother's behavior. Instead of wallowing in self-pity, she forgave her mother and chose to move forward and forge a new relationship with her that ultimately would be a good one. My mom also applied this example when she was figuring the motivations of social climbers, irrational board members, and frightening relatives who wandered into her life.

Armed with a new spirituality, my mom went further into the unconventional by consulting psychics, one of whom mapped out her life, as well as those of her children, with incredible accuracy, noting whom we would marry, when we would have bumps on our journeys, and which career paths we would choose. She had no need to ever look any further. Once she found out that her career would take off in the direction she already knew it would, and the three of us would ultimately be healthy and happy after our idiotic and headstrong choices to follow the rockiest paths possible, there was no need for anything more. Why bother praying for answers or solutions when she knew from the psychic that in the end, all would work out? There was absolutely no practicality in asking the Catholic Church and its God for guidance in such issues since it had already been mapped out for her.

Feeling like she knew the future, in combination with marrying the conventionally Catholic mayor of Los Angeles, short-circuited further curiosity into alternative philosophies. She still kept up the trips to the alternative physician and continued to order large shipments of special ionized water from Japan that was supposed to make her chakras buzz. But being the First Lady of Los Angeles for eight years meant that she generated quite a bit of press. So having the readers of the *Los Angeles Times* learn that she occasionally consulted psychics was probably not the image she—or Dick—wanted to convey. However, she continued some of her avant-garde pursuits at a slower and quieter pace. She was comfortable with what she had learned and preferred to discuss spiritual matters now with her friends on a more casual basis.

Perhaps most importantly, my mom had found what most people search for when it comes to the meaning of their lives: She discovered that what best defined her and made her most content was being directly and strongly connected to her everyday life and the lives of those around her. She no longer needed to search for significance within conventional religion. Her faith and belief lay in her everyday life, that of her family and ultimately her community. She was dedicated to all of us. So, understanding how past lives shaped her decisions as Nancy may have been fun cocktail party conversation but really held little importance when it came to fighting for the things she believed in.

Something my mother and I shared was how problematic Catholicism was for us. But my issues with religion began earlier than my mom's did. Mine started before I was even born. My life began quite differently from those of my brothers. Between 1961, the year my parents got married, and 1966, the year I was born, my parents could not conceive. So they did what Catholics-in-need did back then: They contacted the local Catholic adoption agency, Angel Guardian Home, and placed an order for a child.

On the other side of Brooklyn, a married man working in construction planted his seed into a girl significantly younger. When this young girl found out she was with child, she felt her only choice was to give the baby up for adoption. She was not prepared to be a single mother and was living with a physically and emotionally abusive mother who would never let this baby forget she was a bastard. When the wife of the father found out about the pregnancy, she wanted to adopt the baby and raise it as her own. This was sticky, since the man refused to acknowledge the new child. So the young girl, now doubly certain adoption would be the optimal choice, started her own process at the Angel Guardian Home. The baby was born in February of 1966, went into foster care for nine months, and in November of that year was placed with my parents. That was how my life as Linda Daly began.

So, from my zygote stage to my fat baby-thigh stage, Catholicism complicated my life. One woman's idea of being a good Catholic was to give me up, yet another woman's good Catholic ideals would have put me in a life fraught with lies. I found it so interesting that one religion could polarize people's concepts of "the right thing to do."

While being Catholic had its infinite issues, it was difficult for me to question the existence of God. After all, who had saved me from a Dickensian life in Brooklyn and put me with a really great couple who would give me a life I would always be grateful for? I will never believe that it was a random occurrence.

The excitement of being new parents brought a really wonderful surprise. Shortly after I arrived, my mom became pregnant with my brother Bobby. Three years after that, Brian was born. Our family was complete.

As the children of an Irish Catholic father and a Catholic mother of mixed heritage, my brothers and I were raised in the Church. My parents, however conflicted they were about their religion, followed the direction of generations before them: They brought the family to church, observed the holidays, and didn't question. I do not recall childhood conversations about Catholicism. I find that odd, because it was an essential part of what defined us. As with so many others, it was blind acceptance, an unchangeable part of who we were.

From as early as I can remember, though, being Catholic made little sense to me. There were so many rules that I thought should not apply to people living their everyday lives. From my young perspective it seemed that Catholics were doomed to a life of apologies and guilt. First they're born with Original Sin. How is it possible that a newborn needs to be cleansed of something that might have happened in a creation myth? A simple baptism clears that up, with a lovely brunch to follow, but still. As babies grew into children, they could become little petri dishes of sin without even knowing it. They did stupid things like all kids do—just to see what would happen. However, some of those things were clearly sins, like graffiti, or being a bully. But there were other sins that were marginal, like thinking bad thoughts about someone. God, listening in on kids' evil thoughts about their siblings, can't really take what they say seriously. I was sure He had better things to do, like keeping Hitler in Hell, or making sure there was always music and cherubs in Heaven. To me, my religion held no grey area. Being a card-carrying Catholic meant following arcane rules like confessing your sins, saying daily prayers, and hoping you didn't do something under the radar that you might neglect to confess that would eventually land you in Hell. All the work as a Catholic was to make sure you were cleansed of sins so you could get into Heaven. There wasn't anything about being a good human for the sake of making the most of your life.

As a youngster I was curious about other faiths and their approach to life's big—and little—issues. I knew a little bit about Judaism because half the kids attending my school, Dorchester Elementary in Woodcliff Lake, New Jersey, were Jewish, and our next-door neighbors were Jewish. It struck me as a more alluring religion even then. In temple, they spoke another language. Yiddish words existed for just about everything and were fun to say. They had better food at holidays, went to pray on a Friday night, and didn't have to confess anything regularly or stand in line to receive the body of Christ. They had bar and bat mitzvahs celebrating their entrance into adulthood that included cash prizes. They got to stand up in front of their congregations and be a part of what the adults did. I thought that everything was about the family, coming together to celebrate life and hold on to what was precious. I went to temple once with the neighbors and thought it was so amazing. They had carpet and comfortable seats. There was nothing stark, and everyone chattered throughout the service. I loved the warmth and familiarity of it. It beat church on Sundays and all it entailed, any day.

In my Catholic world, after Mass on Sunday, the kids filed into classrooms to be educated about sins and the rules of

Catholicism. There was conflicting information: God created Eve with Adam's rib, yet men had the same number of ribs as women. Priests ate the body and drank the blood of Jesus Christ Our Savior, yet being a cannibal was a big no-no. We prayed to statues of the Virgin Mary, yet worshiping idols was also supposedly forbidden. Mary Magdalene was a prostitute—bad line of work for a Catholic girl—yet Jesus seemed to like her just fine.

Then there were the sins. I understood the blasphemy of adultery, murder, and stealing things. Those were obvious. But coveting my neighbor's pool and hoping that Dean, the horrible neighbor kid who threw rocks at us, would fall off his bike, break his leg, and get stuck in his house for weeks didn't really seem to qualify as sins. Wasn't it just normal to have those kinds of thoughts? I envied Rhonda Golub's bed since she had a tower of light blue pillows that, back in 1974, was breathtaking. I hated my brothers sometimes. But I wasn't going to kill them or steal Rhonda's pillows.

Frightened by the responsibility of my first communion and my first confession, I was torn with what I should say when it would be my turn to go into the confession box. I didn't think I had a sin worth sharing, but I was afraid to walk into the confessional and have nothing to say. I had to come up with something good, since lying was clearly out of the question. So, after church one Sunday, I walked up to Fusco's, our local deli, slipped a peppermint patty into my pocket, and walked out. I figured stealing something on a Sunday was a decent sin. It was concrete, it was wrong, and with a certain number of Hail Marys and Our Fathers, I'd be good to go.

Heaven perplexed me as well—especially the part about animals not being permitted. Shortly before we moved to California in the summer of 1977, my beloved Samoyed, Lady, was put down. My mom said it was because she was old and couldn't make the trip (which I thought was a lie, but I didn't question it). I asked her if I would see Lady in Heaven. My mom flatly told me that animals don't go to Heaven because they don't have souls. I had that children's Bible with pictures of Jesus in the pastures with all those cute little animals. Those illustrations could not have been Jerusalem; they had to be Heaven. How could my parents raise us in a religion where we weren't going to see our pets in Heaven, and what kind of God wouldn't allow animals to have souls?

Even at my young age, I was angry at the Catholic God because he decided only people gained entrance and only if they were really good. And Purgatory? That seemed worse than Hell, because one had to wait around 'til the laundry list of sins was cleared. The whole thing seemed like a crock. I had all these questions about my religion yet didn't feel comfortable seeking answers. I was fearful that the idea of a question was a sin and dismissive that the "real" God was even paying attention to my plight. Talking to a priest was out of the question because I was convinced I would have to say too many prayers to clear my good name. Instead, I lived with all my conflicts and hoped that someday all my questions would be answered. In the meantime, I would do my best to love and not question God, like Joan of Arc or someone equally impressive.

I think if we had stayed in New Jersey, my religious life would have been very different. I would have gone to Mass with my cousins who lived in the next town over, made it a social event where I would be a part of the community, and raised my future children the way I had been raised. But as fate would have it, my father got a huge promotion and we moved from our comfortable neighborhood in Woodcliff Lake to Los Angeles in 1977. From the research my mother did on schools, the best one in the neighborhood was St. Paul the Apostle School in Westwood. But since there was no room for me in the sixth grade, I went to Warner Avenue until a spot opened up second semester. I joined my brothers there in January of 1978.

The plus side of being in Catholic school meant no Sunday School. However, I thought we kids should be exempt from church altogether since we had religion class every day. Miss Doyle talked about our fire-and-brimstone religion daily, so why would we need to sit through an extra hour on Sundays listening to a priest I could not relate to in the slightest? I argued my case every weekend, asking if we could stay home and watch the televangelists in Orange County instead, to no avail. It's probably no surprise that my first migraine occurred while sitting in church.

Two incidents while I attended St. Paul's ended my relationship with the church. The first came in literature class with Miss Dunne in seventh grade. She was going on about Shakespeare's brilliance and stealthily moved in on the topic of abortion. She said that if Shakespeare's mom had had an abortion, we would never have the great works that we have today. I thought that if God had any sense, and felt these great works were something the human race would enjoy for centuries, He would make sure they would get to us some other way. Maybe William Shakespeare would not have made it into the world, but perhaps some lucky mom down the street would have had a boy whose infinite talent would create the plays we still enjoy today. Or, perhaps those great works were originally intended for some poor soul from a different town and he had died before he was born. Maybe William Shakespeare just happened to be the next baby born and on him were bestowed the talents of the one who didn't make it. I just could not believe that the fates of such masterpieces remained the responsibility of one individual. God had to have something to do with it, and if things were really that important, they'd come out in a different way. That seemed rational to me.

But my true "I am done with Catholicism" epiphany came when the entire eighth-grade class was preparing for our confirmations. This was a huge deal and the ceremony would seal our commitment to the Church. Miss Doyle grilled us on how if we didn't go to church every Sunday from there on out, it would be a sin. We came up with all kinds of scenarios. What if we were on a desert island and there was no church? What if we got into car accidents on the way to church and broke our legs and couldn't get there? What if the church blew up? With every curve ball we threw at her, Miss Doyle repeated the same thing. You would be sinning if you didn't spend an hour on a Sunday in some church somewhere regardless of how many limbs you had left. She did give all of us an out, though: If we were not mature enough to make this commitment, we had the option of not going through the confirmation. Tom Dawson wasn't doing it, but he wasn't Catholic; he was some other kind of Christian. But what eighth grader would have the balls to stand up in front of the entire class and admit they were not mature enough for such a commitment? Certainly not me, an incredibly shy twelve-year-old with no voice whatsoever who was perpetually shrinking into the shadows begging not to be called upon. I couldn't be a rebel when all my friends were doing this. I was petrified of participating, since I knew I couldn't keep this commitment, yet too afraid to stand up and explain myself. I went through with it, got to wear a pretty dress and sing in church. I did live in fear that I would be struck down for my lies to God, but I rationalized that I could explain myself face to face when I had to. God would understand.

After I graduated eighth grade, we left St. Paul's Parish and began attending Good Shepherd in Beverly Hills. This was a delightful relief because it was a smaller church and Ray Bolger—the scarecrow from *The Wizard of Oz*—was one of the ushers. My grandmother, who had moved out to Los Angeles after my grandfather died, liked Good Shepherd as well and we all went to Mass together. One perk was Bagel Nosh around the corner, so after Mass we'd hit the Jewish deli for brunch. We were starting to like church again since Good Shepherd just seemed more relaxed, and most importantly to me, the stained-glass picture windows were more pastoral than those of St. Paul's. So while the priest was giving his sermon, I could daydream my way into being a character on the grassy hill with the sheep.

Just when churchgoing was morphing into a more positive experience, another curve ball was thrown my way. In the early 1980s, my parents' good friends, a Jewish man and a Catholic woman, were going to Castel Gondolfo, the summer residence of Pope John Paul II, for a private audience. They invited my parents to join them. For Catholics, this was the next best thing to meeting God. A blessing from the Pope would surely clear up a lifetime of sins and put you on the fast track to Heaven.

My parents bought all kinds of medallions to be blessed. My mom had a beautiful black suit with a perfect lace veil. They met the Holy See, shook hands, did a little praying, and received their blessing. Perhaps this experience gave my parents the impetus to start dragging us to church again. They came back on a high and talked about how amazing it was to meet the Pope; he was such a nice man. To watch all the people below him waiting for just a glimpse was awe-inspiring stuff. We all wore our medals with pride, and for the first time in a long time, I actually felt closer to God. I felt my cynicism melt away, and I was ready to attend church with a renewed interest. Since I was now driving, I planned on picking up my grandmother so we could share the weekly Mass experience. After all, she was connected to God like no one I've ever met.

But, when my father came home to tell us that the Pope had sent him a screenplay, anything holy and divine about the Pope came crashing to a halt. *The Pope pitched my dad?* I put my medallions away and sulked. How could this happen? Where was the purity of spirit and flowery footpath to Heaven? Like my parents before me, I was struck by how the human side of the Church was interfering with my ability to find a sense of clarity when it came to God.

Church faded from our lives shortly after that, but we continued to go on Christmas, since it was beautiful and the music was wonderful. When I was at my saddest, being there on that night, surrounded by people singing, all the pine, candles, and the life-size crèche were enough to perk my spirits. I even tried to pay attention to the sermons. Sadly, they never said anything that was helpful to me, and eventually it all led back to how we mortals were tragically flawed and had to work so hard to get in God's good graces. There weren't lessons on how to be a better Catholic, just stories about people who were better than we were. If we were to follow by example and not question, we'd be on the right track. Everything I learned was how to lead a clean life so you could be eligible for redemption.

It's safe to say that I wrestled with my faith regularly. I wanted to be closer to God but wasn't sure if leaving Catholicism was the right choice for me. What I really needed to do was divide my faith from my spirituality, but I wasn't sure I could do that without resolving my conflicts with the Church. I had done enough studying to know that the Church had changed dramatically since the time of Christ. I knew bureaucracy had taken over what had been simple faith. I was aware of the Church's history of violence in the name of God and how much money the Vatican controlled. All this should have made it easier for me to be an independent thinker, but I always lived with the fear that God was really Catholic and I would burn in Hell for all the things I was thinking.

So I went through college, dated an Irish Catholic like myself, and felt no closer to God, since he was about as religious as I was. I dated an agnostic and felt even less. I started reading Edgar Cayce and expanding my mind to a broader realm of spirituality. I studied Native American culture, trying to figure out what fit. I checked out Buddhism, Islam, Presbyterianism, and Unitarianism, but nothing really stuck. I read about astrology, tried to get in touch with my psychic side. I consulted a Sikh about reading auras and got into the New Age crap of the nineties. But that ultimately wasn't my thing either. My parents divorced during this time as well. Neither of them cared about how it looked in the eyes of the Church. I didn't understand why I had such religious conflicts if they did not.

I unhappily decided to cross religion off my list altogether when I married my first husband, Eddy, a Jew. We planned on having kids and raising them to be good Jews, just like my childhood neighbors. At that point, no one in my family cared what religion was in the house. My grandmother had died earlier that year, and any questions she would have raised were buried with her. My father had moved in with Carole, who was Jewish, and my mom and Dick were living in sin. To paraphrase the great Bob Weir, we were going to Hell in a bucket, baby, but at least we were enjoying the ride.

For our wedding, Eddy and I decided on a Jewish ceremony and found a rabbi who would marry a shiksa and a Jew. It was a beautiful wedding. Eddy became a temple member at his synagogue, Wilshire Boulevard Temple, and I attended High

Holiday services with him. I started to memorize the music during Kol Nidre and began to feel at peace, knowing one day Wilshire would be my community for many years to come.

Like many Reform Jews, Eddy was only mildly observant. I don't recall us ever discussing his closeness to God, but we did talk about his very strong feelings about his religious identity. He attended High Holiday services because it was what one was supposed to do, but Eddy was more secular than religious. To him, it was important to keep the faith so the Jewish identity would be passed down to the kids. The ritual of lighting the Shabbat candles, saying the prayers, and spending time with family was most important. His family was a mixed bag of observance. His sister and her family were very active in their synagogue in New York, but his brother in Denver had no religious identity whatsoever. It seems Eddy got his identity from his mother, who always prepared beautiful holiday dinners and made the best gefilte fish I've ever tasted. On the flip side, his dad had not one ounce of spirituality about him.

When discussing raising the kids with religion, Eddy didn't care if I converted. I felt conversion was out of the question. Since I had yet to resolve my conflicts with the religion I was born into, I felt I had no business taking on another. That changed when, five months into my first pregnancy, I waddled into my mother's house to see a friend of hers who had come to town. Donald Cohen was the head of the Yale Child Study Center and one of the pioneers of the study of autism and early childhood behavior. He was on the National Children's Commission with my mom under the first Bush Administration and happened to be a very spiritual Jew.

The day I stopped by for a visit, he asked me in which faith we would be raising the children. Without hesitation, I said Jewish. He said I couldn't because I was still Catholic. When

I told him I had no intention of converting, that I wanted to figure out my own religion first, he replied, "Kids have a hard enough time growing up. Make it easy on them. If you don't convert and you're raising them in a religion you won't accept as your own, what kind of message are you sending?" I was also unaware that unless I converted, my kids would not technically be Jewish. Their religious identity had to come from their mother.

Donald was someone whose opinion on faith I respected. Once when my mother and I were in New Haven for a Yale conference on children's issues, we had dinner at their house during Sukkot. I learned about the sukkah and liked the idea of celebrating the harvest, embracing the fragility of life, and holding it dear. I connected with this family and their religion and thought, hmm . . . maybe this one is for me. They asked questions, thought things out, had descriptions for holidays, praying, and existing as a Jew and a human that I never had as a Catholic.

For the sake of the big baby in my belly and whatever future siblings he might have, I made an appointment that day with the young rabbi at Wilshire Boulevard and began my conversion. Of course, the chance to get a clean start in the faith department was an equal factor in this decision. I went to conversion classes, and I had private tutoring with the rabbi where I was able to question the scripture without feeling like I was doing something wrong. I learned about Tikkun Olam, repairing the world, and Gemilut Hasadim, acts of loving kindness. This was a religion I could understand. It fit the kind of person I was. All my volunteering was not to get myself a better place in line for the pearly gates—it was to help others and feel good about it in the process. No guilt, no ulterior motives, just wanting to give time and energy and write a few checks to make the world a better place. So, at nine months pregnant, I crossed my fingers and hoped that the Catholic God would forgive me as I dunked my head under the mikvah waters three times to become a Jew.

My parents didn't seem to mind that I had converted to Judaism; I think they were pleased that I had figured out what would make me happy. When my son, Leo, was born, we participated in the religious rituals one must do as a Jew. Leo was circumcised at his bris, surrounded by our families and closest friends. As tradition dictated, Eddy and Leo's godfather buried Leo's foreskin under a tree. When Julianna was born seventeen months later, tradition called for a baby naming where Julianna was officially inducted into the House of Judaism. We were now a little Jewish family, and I made challah on Friday nights in anticipation of Shabbat. Eddy's mom came over for those Shabbat dinners, and we became close with our rabbi. The kids went to preschool at the temple. We were living a lovely Jewish life.

Even as our religion was solid, the marriage was not. Eddy and I were not good spouses to each other, and eventually we divorced. Nothing dramatic happened; it was just a slow deterioration until there was nothing left but resentment. The divorce was quick, and neither of us asked for more than we deserved by law. We divided some of the property; he kept the house, and I was able to buy a cozy cottage in Brentwood. Eddy and I successfully moved past one of the most difficult times in our lives, remaining friendly enough to always share funny things that happened with the kids. Divorce just meant we weren't living in the same house anymore and were free to fall in love with other people. That one vow of " 'til death do you part" would hold true forever, though, because we would always share our children. We made the best of it, and still do.

In spite of the losses I experienced during that time, I found a deeper sense of community with our temple, which in turn led to a deeper spirituality. My rabbi spoke to me often about what was happening in my life and assured me that if I dropped Eddy's last name from mine, my identity in the temple community would be just as strong. I got a position teaching art at the religious school and continued my involvement in the congregation.

My closest friends were moms from the preschool who remained by my side throughout the divorce. I was able to become a person with a voice.

I headed up the newly formed social action committee with the new incoming rabbi, Stephen Julius Stein. We were asked to try to change the culture of the temple into one engaged in our community and beyond. Rabbi Stein and I organized congregation-wide volunteer days to send a shipping container filled with school supplies to children in Darfuri refugee camps and a few pallets of personal grooming supplies to Hurricane Katrina victims. Through my work on the social action committee, I became more interested in humanitarian work. I visited refugee camps in Chad, met women dying of AIDS, and saw some of the worst poverty on the planet. All of it deepened my connection to our planet and developed a stronger sense of my Jewish identity. For a while, I began to see my full potential as a human through Judaism. But I was looking for something more. I had no idea what it was, but that old feeling of not being close to God was creeping up again. I began to wonder if being a member of an organized religion might not actually be for me.

I was still working at the ranch full-time and was thrilled to discover that my sense of spirituality returned when I was in the garden with my hands in the earth or listening to the bees work the pollen out of the cucumber flower. My stress would lighten up as I would drive through Malibu Canyon, where I could see the many layers of rock that had been thrust up from ancient glaciers. The beauty of these striations would be the entrance to my inner peace. Entering the ranch, hearing the crunch of gravel under my tires and the excited panting of my dogs led to this crescendo of warm peace. My silent routine began with seeing what had grown overnight. Walking down to the garden, I would watch the dogs zing by me, tails wagging as they searched desperately for ground squirrels. Nothing could hold back a smile as I began my day looking for new vegetables. It was here that I could escape any negativity in my life, start listening to my breathing, and feel a lightness that I equated with feeling closer to God. I was around animals and discovered that they have more soul than most humans. Yet even when I was at my most peaceful, on horseback, watching the marine layer cascade down the mountains, the conflict remained. Why could I not get this feeling when I was around other people who were all together worshipping a God they loved?

I was searching again, but for what, I didn't know.

By now, it was late 2007. My mom had been sick for a year and a half. While I was working hard to not let my mother's illness consume me, it was starting to engulf me entirely. I had received a job offer from a start-up web company that would allow me to write professionally about philanthropy. My week was divided into quiet reflective time at the ranch and active, creatively inspiring days with colleagues that excited me. When I wasn't wrapped up in being concerned that I was taking on too much again, I was questioning why God would allow my mom, doer of only good deeds, to become so sick. I tried to look for the lessons and see the bigger picture, but it was difficult. No matter what, my mom was going to die and miss out on the amazing things that would happen in our family. I was alone, living with intense sadness, yet raising two amazing children who continued to bring me joy every day. I was volunteering when I could and trying not to drown too many of my sorrows in french fries or dark chocolate. I hadn't made it past a first date in four years and was convinced that my inner turmoil was leaching out, forcing any potential suitor to head screaming for the hills. I was on the verge of becoming the crazy lady on the block with corn in her front yard and too many dogs.

Christmas of that year, I was facing a holiday alone. My children were with their dad on some fabulous tropical vacation. My mother and Dick were in Sun Valley, my dad and Carole were in New York, and my brothers had their own plans. I was about to settle in on the couch with a handful of movies when my friend called to say they were throwing together an impromptu orphans holiday dinner. She and her husband had decided not to travel back to his family this year, and it turned out they had friends who had decided to stay home as well. So we all got together and decided to make dinner for ourselves and play Guitar Hero. Dressed in sweats and loaded with ingredients for my polenta, I headed out, actually feeling a little hopeful.

It was at this dinner that my life took the most fabulous turn. It was one of those moments of true revelation that I thought happened only in fiction. In other words: I fell in love at first sight with someone I had known for years. As I was stirring my polenta, I was deep in conversation with my friend Mike, who always made me laugh, and another guest, who decided at that moment to share his interest in leaving his current job as a mortgage broker to venture into Hollywood. I couldn't listen anymore to this guy talk about switching from a stable career to one fraught with uncertainty. So I turned back to the stove and heard Mike explain to the guy in the kindest of terms that his plan was not very sound. I turned to look at Mike, and it struck me that this cute and very dear man, perpetually clad in sweater vests, was going to be the one who would calmly explain to my children that they should think things through before jumping into something they may regret later. I wasn't one to sugarcoat anything and was smart enough to know I would eventually need someone to balance my calling a spade a spade. Mike would be the right person to counter my occasional bad parenting with his even-tempered good nature. Ironic, too, because from what I knew of Mike, he didn't want children; nor did he ever want to get married. It was my first moment of blind faith. I had complete confidence from that moment that I had found not only the man of my dreams but someone who would take equal delight in my children. Mike was someone who would embody our family motto: embrace the wackiness.

I decided that night that he was the man I would be with for the rest of my life. All of that "getting to know you" stuff and the dredging out of skeletons was unnecessary because we'd been friends for about seven years. He and the kids hit it off immediately. We were together for about nine months before we started to talk seriously about marriage. A few weeks before Thanksgiving of 2008, we went ring shopping.

We drove up to Healdsburg in Sonoma County, the Friday morning after Thanksgiving, for a weekend getaway of excellent food and vineyard visits. We had been in our hotel room for about an hour, talking about how certain we were that we'd be together forever, when he popped the question. It couldn't have been more perfect. Mike has been with me through the darkest time of my life, steady and strong. He'd made me laugh and had allowed me to find joy in life again. I adored and treasured everything about him. He understood having a sick parent, since his mom had died of colon cancer in 2000.

Upon arrival in Los Angeles, we wasted no time picking a date. Since we knew we wanted a low-key outdoor wedding, we optimistically picked late August out at my dad's ranch, hoping that my mother would be well enough to participate. It was an obvious choice for me, and Mike loved it there as much as I did. The lawn sprawled on forever, and we could be safe from the heat under a small grove of mature oaks deep down in the property.

But those plans changed as we rounded the corner past my birthday in February. My mother was becoming weaker each day. Her cancer had advanced to the point where none of us were sure my mom would still be around in August. She was rapidly declining and at this point was not eating much more than ice cream. She was sleeping more, becoming forgetful, and was in more pain than ever before. Our whole family was at a birthday brunch for Carole in early March, when we discussed moving the date so we could ensure my mother's presence at the wedding. We changed the entire plan, deciding to have a small family-only ceremony in our backyard and save the August date for a reception.

Even though Mike and I were relieved to have made this decision, we were afraid to talk to my mom about it. Fearful she'd get mad if we told her we didn't think she'd make it that long, we came up with another story. We decided to tell her that we were moving up the date of the ceremony because having the wedding at the same time as the reception was edging out of our price range. It seemed reasonable to me. My dad and Carole decided to come with us to break the news to my mom. Mike and I needed backup, and my dad and Carole would be able to break any tension that would develop if my mom insisted on not changing anything on her behalf.

So we all sat in the den of the house she bought once her divorce was final and told her the new plan. She thought about it for a second and plainly asked if it was because of her. I said that it was. I couldn't lie to her; it was so evident that she was too ill to make it out of the house most days. Even though the code with my mom was not to cry and treat things lightly, I just couldn't not. What should have been the happiest moment of my life with Mike was shrouded in sadness and uncertainty. So I opened the floodgates and cried in front of everyone.

Once I started I couldn't stop.

All the fear I had that my mom would die spilled forth in front of me. I dared to utter the words *cancer* and *death* in the same sentence. My mom was just as sad, knowing that what I was saying was the truth. There were lots of tears shed by all of us as we chose the following weekend to have our ceremony. None of us wanted to waste any time, and I was on the edge of a breakdown. The reality of her being gone was all too present at that moment, and I had to use all the strength I had to continue getting out of bed and pretending to be a functioning human being. The dichotomy of being happy and sad at the same time was exhausting.

Rabbi Stein married Mike and me in our backyard under the chuppah. Mike was in a cream suit; I was barefoot, in a light green spring dress. The dogs were there, all clean with big pretty bows. My son, Leo, invoking the family motto, was in costume and led the processional playing his recorder. Julianna was in a beautiful red dress and carried flowers. It was delightful except for one thing: My mom was dying.

Technically, Mike was Jewish, although religion played no part in his life. Most of his religious references came from *Jesus Christ Superstar* or *Fiddler on the Roof*. His mom was Jewish; her family were Holocaust survivors who fled Germany and settled in Stockholm. Mike's dad was an atheist raised in Kentucky now married to an Evangelical Christian. Odd, but it worked for both parties. Mike had the lightness of someone with no religious baggage. He was never burdened with Jewish guilt, the existence of a judgmental God, or questions about whether he'd go to Heaven or Hell. Mike was always open to discussing God but had no point of reference when it came to my obsession with spirituality. He listened always, didn't try to solve anything, and didn't tell me what to think. He was present through my constant conversations about searching for something deeper but had no interest in any kind of quest for himself. In that journey, I was on my own.

Being the levelheaded person he is, Mike listened patiently to my one-sided discussions on my search for more spirituality, religion, and God. My mom's illness and the drama that surrounded it, plus trying to keep the balance between a normal life with two young children and a joyful relationship with Mike, had my head in a spin.

In tears one night while I was brushing my teeth, my ever-patient husband listened to my lunacy. I was letting myself spin out of control. I entertained the notion that my mom's cancer would be the catalyst to get me back on the spirituality track. Selfish as it seemed, I really wanted to get something out of this situation. I'd been dealing with this disease for more time than anyone should. I willingly put everything aside for my mom, and I did not want to accept the possibility that I was only just the dutiful daughter/tour guide. I wanted to believe there was more in it for me, that God would reward me in ways I couldn't imagine.

Nothing sucked more than watching my mother deteriorate. I wanted a positive experience for which I could be grateful. It appeared, at this point, that we were both looking for a miracle cure. And with this line of thought it became evident that I was in a deeper spiritual crisis than I realized.

| CHAPTER FOUR |

While I was having my crisis of faith, my mom was in a crisis of fashion. Every season for as long as I remember, she had a few select Rodeo Drive boutiques deliver the new collections for viewing. Even in the midst of her illness, the deliveries continued. She also had connections at the major department stores for shoes and handbags, because, as she said, "One should always have the leathers matching." She shopped like she was going to live forever. Which of course she was not.

Since a fair amount of my mother's energy was spent on fashion, it made sense that her center of power was her closet. When she was well, it was where her closest friends came to dish and where the female members of the family congregated to try on shoes, jewelry, and makeup and marvel at her exquisitely embroidered Oscar de la Renta handbags. This continued well into her illness. She spent hours in this extremely large, pink marbled and mirrored annex, pulling any restorative energy she could from the beauty surrounding her. Her frail frame teetered in new shoes from the top designers with the intention of wearing them to the season openings of the L.A. Opera and the L.A. Philharmonic. More often than not, there was a girlfriend sitting on the plush carpeted floor, talking to my mom about the town's happenings.

My mother was always impeccably dressed, even if she was just on her way to chemo. As her illness progressed, however, she downgraded from Chanel suits to Juicy Couture. Regardless of her ensembles, Nancy looked ready for anything as she entered her doctor's office. We may have thought her delusional for buying all those clothes, but for her, life was not even close to being over. I know this attitude kept her going well past her expiration date. She was just too busy to die, even though her body was deteriorating by the hour.

By late summer of 2009, she weighed less than ninety-five pounds and had to have her size zero clothing taken in even more. Since my mother had the incredible ability to make the best of a dire situation, she created an opportunity for herself to acquire more cashmere wraps and sweaters since her low body fat was making her cold all the time. For all the new things she bought, she had a ready disclaimer: "If I don't get to wear these," she would say to me, "some day these will be yours." I knew it meant only the shoes, though, since I was sizing up as she was sizing down.

It was evident to me at this time that her life was winding down. Physically, the cancer was taking over, even though she would never discuss the progress of her disease. Mentally, though, she remained focused on her life and how she was going to make the most of every day, to the point where she was actually becoming a challenge to those supporting her. As the cancer swept through her body, she fought to remain independent. One of her first acts of defiance was refusing the care of a full-time nurse. She was adamant that she did not need anyone taking care of her. Admitting she actually required more help was a sign her life was close to over. She was also incredibly proud. This pride prevented her from seeing the truth in her situation that she really was not all right being left alone at night.

All the chemo, pain medication, and insulin adjustments took away her ability to think properly. She forgot what she was saying, was tired all the time, and had a hard time following a conversation. Everything was taxing for her, so we did our best to hang out in her bedroom so she could stay in bed. We pretended her room was the better one to watch movies, so she could nap and take as many conversation breaks as she needed. Melida was also reporting that my mom wandered around at night, and Melida was afraid she would fall or become disoriented in the dark. My mom had gotten into the habit of sleeping most of the afternoon and being wide awake at 3:00 am. Her patterns had shifted so dramatically as we thought her body was doing its darnedest to fight. As a result, Melida insisted on sleeping at my mom's, taking only Sunday nights off so she could tend to her own ailing mother.

Since my mom loved Melida as much as Melida loved her, we leveraged Melida's well-being to convince my mom to finally get a nurse. However, once she agreed, my mom came up with a set of rules for the nurse that would allow my mom to retain some control over her situation. Some of them included the nurse not being allowed into my mom's room when she was sleeping, not following her too closely on the stairs, not hovering while she was eating, and generally blending into the curtains until it was time to check her insulin or give her meds—which my mother wanted to keep in her bathroom. Fortunately, we convinced her that these rules would actually prevent the nurse from being helpful if an emergency arose. We also spoke to the nurses on the side to tell them to ignore most of what my mom was saying. We were all so concerned that her forgetfulness would lead to an overdose on her insulin. Having a professional in the house that could take care of any emergency made us all feel a lot better.

Even with the additional support, Melida was hesitant to leave my mom alone. She also didn't want the nurse to have to tiptoe around my mother, who would invariably yell, thinking she was being monitored too closely. So Melida teamed up with the nurse and watched the downstairs, like she had all this extra organizing to do for my mom. She ended up staying each night until 10:00 pm, just to make sure everything was copacetic. Melida used to sit in the kitchen late at night when my mom was wandering the house, watching the security monitor to make sure she didn't go outside. On more than one occasion, she reported that the camera outside my mother's window and the one that showed the front door had ghostly white wispy things that flew around my mother's windows. She was convinced my mom was going to die soon and that these were ghosts that were going to make sure she got to Heaven.

My mother then decided she was no longer arguing with anyone. Instead, she would say yes to everything presented to her. Either she was forgetting what was happening or she had become quite sly in her tactics to keep us all satisfied that she was listening to us. As a result, when those around her would compare notes, someone would end up becoming confused, and I would get a call to find out the straight story. We had landed ourselves back in the days of her being in the hospital with us needing to do damage control. It was exhausting trying to keep a lid on the plans she would make for herself when she had already decided to do something else. Our web of communication around her was constant. Her girlfriends would call me to share exciting news my mom had shared with them on a treatment, or how she was feeling so much better and would be able to meet them for dinner soon. I was the one who had to break the news that nothing had changed, and she was never awake past 5:00 AM anymore, so if they wanted to see her, they should come over late morning, when she had the most energy.

When it came to my brothers and me, we decided we should speak daily to make sure we all had any new information straight and then secure that with a conversation with Rita. We were never sure when Mom said yes to one of us if it meant plans with another would be usurped. Sometimes we would call her on becoming the Queen of Yesses but realized it was fruitless, since she pretended not to know what we were talking about or simply just plain forgot. Either way, having a mom in this stage was not only frustrating, it was incredibly sad. I could only imagine this is what it would have been like if she had been stricken by dementia.

Her increasingly frustrating behavior also included her being less than honest with the nurses about when she took her medications and what she ate and when. She was no longer capable of monitoring her own intake and care. Unfortunately, it was everyone else's fault. When she wasn't complaining to us about how Melida didn't think she was eating enough—which she wasn't—she resented my brothers and me for wanting to know what was going on at her house. She thought we were hovering too much as well.

She begged to be left alone with her nutty little Yorkie, Lily, who had decided it was her sole mission to protect my mother from anything that posed a threat. This included gardeners, any animals on TV, squirrels, and small children who ran up the stairs to my mother's room. She wanted to sit in her bathroom, watch TV, and try on clothing while thinking about lunches she would host so she could wear all the new ensembles. Not quite Norma Desmond, but getting closer by the day.

I guess she had to think of something other than dying, since reality was no fun anymore. That we understood.

It wasn't long after that the night nurse turned into a round-the-clock gig, even if it was just for our peace of mind. We felt even better knowing Melida would be let off the hook and someone would be able to administer the right amount of insulin if my mom opted for dulce de leche ice cream over a warm bowl of vegetable soup.

In calmer moments, my mother decided her health care was not sufficient. She disliked her doctor because he didn't check in with her enough. I have no way of knowing if this was true, but when I spoke to him about it at my mother's request, when he did call, she always said she was feeling all right and there wasn't anything she needed from him. It felt like she would do or say anything to shift the blame of the disease's progression. She begged me to call my internist to see if he would take on her case. When I had that conversation with him, he declined, saying he wouldn't take on someone as ill as my mother. He also taught with my mother's internist, so running into him would make things rather awkward.

I can only imagine how sad and desperate she was feeling knowing her life was cascading closer to death. While it was hard to feel anything but frustration towards her for her resentful behavior, I gave her a lot of slack. I don't know who she was being truthful to about how she was really feeling, and I wasn't convinced she was telling anyone how she truly felt, since I never heard from her closest friends that she complained about anything. My mom's Barbie attitude was shining through, her painful smile trying harder and harder to look convincing. So, always with deep breaths, I would continue my check-ins with her and then Rita, just to let my mom know I was still watching her back.

₂ℓₑ

We were approaching fall of 2009. Having a nurse full-time was one sort of relief. But the stress was becoming greater on other levels. We continued to have family dinners at her house, but my mom participated less and less. She would make a plate of food, sit with us for a few minutes, push her food around, and maybe take one bite. I was coming up with flavorful ways to make her food better without adding heat. She could not tolerate any pepper, since the chemo had made the inside of her mouth so sensitive. I was sneaking white beans into pesto sauce, hoping the extra fiber and protein would benefit her. Tofu was blended into pureed vegetable soups as well. It was like feeding Leo when he was little.

Invariably, she would get up and make a bowl of ice cream for herself and we would all sigh, knowing if we said anything she would go upstairs and wait for us to leave. We were desperate for her to have something nutritious, but she couldn't eat anything more than a cold sweet dessert. We didn't know this was a telltale sign.

One of the bright spots in my mother's otherwise dreary weeks was her time with her best friend, Joanne. She was taking my mom for weekly facials and shopping trips, all centered on ice cream shops around the city. They would hire someone to drive them around so they could sit in the back and chitchat about anything of interest. It was cherished time for both of them. My mom would get her pampering, she'd buy a new scarf or a piece of jewelry, and then they would go all out on some sundae. She would always come home a little brighter, having laughed, eaten what she wanted without anyone judging her, and with a new purchase to show us.

I loved seeing my mom either leave for or come back from one of her trips with Joanne. I got to see the little sparkle that was left. It was the only time she was carefree.

Since giving up on Western medicine, my mom was taking care of other angles, especially since her last round of chemo had greatly reduced her quality of life. It did extensive damage to every aspect of her: It took away her energy, made her violently ill, and caused random pain that kept her on pain medicine that made her loopy. It was a natural segue for her to make appointments with healers. So she piled them on. She had a Chinese healer come to do cranial sacral work and readjust her chakras and her aura. She had a reflexologist who applied tremendous pressure to parts of her bony feet to stimulate her immune system. She also had two other rather sly and aggressive healers come to lay their hands on her. They were particularly annoying to me because they insisted on spending more and more time with my mom. They never asked for money but constantly hinted how donations would certainly help their cause.

My mom had taken all the suggestions people had previously given her about alternative cures and had healers come in one by one. The ones she liked, she had come more often, sometimes having different people come within the same day. She thought of it as insurance. We were in no position to say anything about her interest; we figured she should do whatever made her feel good. Even with the consistent refrain of breathing in the healing light, there still was one option she wished she had chosen earlier in her cancer.

Soon after she got back from Johns Hopkins, someone had suggested an outlandish yet intriguing idea to my mother. For a while, we had mildly entertained the idea of going to Brazil to see the renowned healer John of God. My mom and I, then seasoned travelers in developing nations, enthusiastically talked about what it would be like to go there. Rita even got in on constructing a preliminary itinerary for us. We thought it would be a fascinating visit. My mom and I casually discussed who would be the best candidates to accompany us. We went through her list of girlfriends, crossing off one after the other because we knew this sort of trip would be similar to going to Africa. We did decide that the two people who could rough it for the greater spiritual good would be Carole and Tim. Carole was the most spiritual person we knew. Roughing it was not her forte, but for something as extraordinary as this, we had a feeling she would roll with the punches. Tim would not only be a blast but would take it seriously and would probably get as much out of it as we would. This trip would be a ten-day ordeal. One of the bigger obstacles was trying to coordinate dates. Another was locating private transportation into the wilds of Brazil.

For as exciting as it sounded early on, the motivation waned as my mother's health improved.

While my mom was in her first round of chemo, she and her reflexologist had a deep discussion about John of God. The reflexologist went to see him annually. She brought down photos of friends and clients who were ill so John of God could bless them. She happened to be going down the following month so offered to take one of my mom's pictures with her. Not missing a beat, when the session was over, my mom handed over a picture of herself from a healthier and happier time, gave the reflexologist a hug, and hoped to be feeling better shortly. When my mom told me about the picture, I was actually disappointed. Even though the reflexologist claimed it was common practice and the next best thing to actually going herself, I was hoping we could make the trip. John of God would be blessing the picture instead of my mom, and somehow all the healing vibes would travel through the image of my mother and into her soul. I definitely raised an eyebrow at this proposal, more because I felt let down about the shortcut to a supposed cure. But my mom was feeling better. And realistically, this kind of trip was more than she wanted to do. Having her picture blessed could be enough.

While the trip to Brazil had been short-circuited, I had secretly become fascinated by its possibilities and thought I could convince my mom later on to actually go. First, I was always up for an international adventure. Second, traveling with my mom was always fun. Third, I'd not been to South America, and what better way to see a country than to go deep into it for a spiritual pilgrimage. Being someone who is perpetually fascinated by faith and how far that alone can be responsible for healing the mind and body, I wanted to see this in action. The whole idea of this trip could be a boon for how I was feeling about my own spirituality. After Africa, which was a great bonding trip, I thought Brazil would hold an even greater potential for us to become even closer. Experiencing a healing moment for my mom, or for me, could only result in us having a significant experience.

I did the most extensive search on John of God that I could when the initial conversation began. I had heard of him before. The news show *20/20* did a piece on him that captivated me. However, there was not much to find through my expert Internet

searches. There were some testimonials of pilgrims, some articles on how no one could explain why his magic worked. And
then there were the videos of what were called psychic surgeries,
where he would literally cut into people while they were in a
trance and "remove" whatever ailed them. He seemed rather
mythical. Even with all of this so-called evidence of his abilities,
I was not convinced. I wanted hard evidence from a normal
person that John of God was who he said he was. Throughout
my mom's cancer, I continued my quest for more information. I
knew the chances of us going were remote no matter how good
she felt. However, I held on to the idea that someday I might go
myself. As time moved on, interestingly enough, upon entering
"John of God" into Google, I got a lot more information than
I had before.

Born João Teixeira da Faria on June 24, 1942, John of God
was clairvoyant as a child. He began his spiritual/surgical career when he was sixteen, even though he had only two years
of formal education. After being fired as a tailor's apprentice,
he went for a swim in a nearby creek, where he had a vision
of a conversation with Saint Rita of Cascia, the patron saint of
impossible causes.

Saint Rita told him to visit a church in town, because people
were expecting him. Upon arrival, he lost consciousness. João
awoke in the church, thinking he had passed out from hunger.
But church members say he had channeled the spirit of King Sol-
omon, healed many people, and performed surgeries. Throughout his career as a healer, he managed to gather a bunch of
spirit advisors. Known as the Entities, these spirits were doctors
from previous centuries who would advise him on how to cure
whomever he encountered. He went on to become one of the
most talked-about healers of our times, according to the websites I visited.

John of God claims it is God, not he, allowing the Entities to assist him in healing whoever comes to call. It is also stated plainly on many of the websites I visited that there is not a one-time healing. If you visit John of God at the Casa Dom Inácio in the town of Abadiânia, you get about ten seconds in his presence each of the days you're advised to be there. Visitors get his blessing and then are left to go to work to fix their own problems. They can lie on "crystal beds" to help the healing process, sit in "current rooms" where the Entities are always at work, or meditate on the grounds. Bottom line, if you want to be healed, you have to do the work. That work includes an additional forty days of no sex, pork, pepper, or alcohol. Apparently, they all weaken the body's aura.

Visitors to the Casa can have invisible surgeries on what ails them. This means the Entities work without the help of João. However, if you're lucky or brave enough and between the ages of eighteen and fifty-two, you can ask for a psychic surgery. To me, these were quite terrifying to watch. John of God is guided by the Entities and removes something that is not supposed to be in your body. In some of the videos, he sticks something up someone's nose and pulls out a bloody chunk. It looks horrifying, but the "patients" claim to not feel a thing. Another video showed a woman having her breast cut open with a scalpel as John of God dug around and pulled out a bloody mass. How he knows what to do and what to pull out of people's bodies is beyond me and definitely something I was not interested in having my mother experience. My guess is he doesn't perform these surgeries when he ventures into other countries, which he does all the time. The U.S. Federal Trade Commission described them in the late '70s as a complete hoax.

Still, even though I was now thoroughly skeptical and grossed out, I became hooked. I watched a few more videos.

He touched eyeballs, cut more people to pull out lumps, shoved surgical clamps up noses. It was all so questionable and daring, yet not one person complained. There was no reported infection even though there was nothing remotely sterile about his work. No pain was experienced by anyone. It was all a little much, but it held my attention like a car accident. I just wanted to see how bad it really was.

After overloading on videos, I had become quite cynical about this entire prospect. It had the aura of a circus side show where the "patients" were really actors and the surgeries were sleight-of-hand to make John of God look all-powerful. Now, I just wanted to prove that none of this was real. But there was something else I thought about in regards to my fantasy trip with my mother. She had a deadly illness; she wanted to be cured, no matter what. I wasn't sure that my mother could do the remaining work recommended by the Casa. She still had not become the spiritual guru she had intended once her cancer had gone into remission after her first chemo.

I discovered a few logistical negatives that could shut the book on entertaining the fantasy of visiting John of God. It was not easy to get there, and someone in compromised health would have serious difficulty. So if my mom made the trip and fell ill, there was no real MD there to tend to her. If the worst happened and she died there, it would be extraordinarily difficult to get her back to the States. Getting there was also quite expensive, approximately $7,000 per person. Also, you couldn't just show up there and expect to be taken care of. There were "Casa Approved" guides from the U.S. and Canada who led groups down there for healing, and they were asking $1,800 or so per person, according to the official John of God website. Lodging—which was in addition to the cost of the guide— ran between $150 and $250 a night. And there was also the nominal $40 cost per person for a visa, not to mention the fee for the bus that took you from the Aeroporto Internacional de Brasília. For all the cash being dished out, the accommodations weren't even going to be anything close to those at the Four Seasons. There was only so much pilgrimaging anyone in *this* group was prepared to do.

So, for all the research and planning, thoughtful evaluation and hopeful turnouts, I had let go of any ideas of a pilgrimage. Even though it appealed to me to visit the presence of such a strong faith healer, it was just too far out of reach. My mother was in no shape to walk around the block, let alone fly to Brazil. In my quieter moments, I questioned how the trip might change me—and interestingly enough, that alone made me nervous about going. I would be in the presence of someone who had such an incredible impact on others, so if I allowed myself to really be open, I had the possibility of feeling a deeper sense of spirituality and maybe even feeling closer to God. Whether or not John of God's claims were for real was not for me to judge until I actually got to see him face to face. I judged myself harshly on this and questioned if I had the will to do the work needed to fix my own ailing spirit. When I started to look at this possibility from a more spiritual perspective, I wondered if my mother's interest in this was actually meant for *my* cure.

With this line of thought, it became clear that I was losing my marbles. My growing confusion over the "right way" to be spiritual was compounded by a new discovery: how my spiritual health hinged on my time outdoors in the garden. I had guilt that I was more at peace in the presence of bees and growing vegetables than I was participating in Jewish traditions and rituals. I started to beat myself up over the possibility that I had wasted my time becoming a Jew, since going to temple was doing nothing more than making me feel like I didn't belong.

I had grown up with such rules on how I was supposed to feel connected to God. My judgment had become so clouded with this possible John of God visit. I wasn't feeling secure enough in my chosen religion to make the leap to the possibilities of a Christian healer and didn't know where any religion fit into my need to be in the garden. My black-and-white personality just didn't allow for all these conflicting ways to feel connected to mesh together.

In the beginning of 2009, I had made a decision about my mental health. My mother's cancer was getting the better of me, so I had to take control over whatever I could. I was gaining weight and showing signs of depression. I was sleepless, lacked energy, and could not wait to get into bed every night. I was snapping at my children and stopped talking to friends about how I was feeling. I was slipping into a darker place every day and became frightened about who I was becoming. So I applied for a position in the Los Angeles County Master Gardener Program.

Only fifty people were accepted to this rigorous program each year. I held great hopes that I would be able to become grounded again with more education about gardening and would take advantage of everything this program had to offer. Being a Master Gardener meant that I could choose a garden project, teach lower-income Angelenos to grow their own food, and become part of a state-wide network of people hell bent on turning every available space into a haven for homegrown produce. These people cherished the earth as much as I did. I already knew being in the garden was good medicine for me, so spending time with others like me could only be a good thing.

The anticipation of that acceptance was like waiting for my college letters. I was so excited about it. I held such validation in this acceptance and vowed to take it all seriously. It was going to be a huge commitment, ten Saturdays from nine to four, in a county building on Cesar Chavez Boulevard off the 710 freeway in East Los Angeles. From the second I walked into that door, I knew I was with my people. There were a bunch of people in Birkenstocks and socks and natural fibers. I smiled as wide as I could and found a seat. I knew from the equally grateful smiles of those around me that this would be even better than I thought.

I could escape once a week to a place where my mom's cancer didn't factor into anything. I could escape my sadness and focus on learning.

It occurred to me partway through this program that I may have found my religion and my people. Every week, we opened our big books to a different chapter. We listened to the words spoken and all had interpretations of what we should do with them. Sometimes I knew more than others, but other times I felt like I knew nothing. The sharing of experiences and methods was enlightening. I learned from some serious professionals that a good gardener is measured by failure. I could identify with that, since every year the cumulative knowledge about tomatoes made me think even further outside the box on how to properly care for them. This new community was blooming and I was an active member. I would leave every session feeling my spirit lifting. The dark hole of depression that may have swallowed me shrank every time I completed a class. I should have been tired, but I was energized with the possibilities of finding a different path to spirituality. Driving home, I wondered if I could assuage my guilt for finding the key to my happiness. Wasn't religion supposed to do that for me?

I found myself in an extraordinary predicament. I was still enmeshed in my Jewish community, finding spirituality in East L.A. with my garden buddies, and fantasizing about a pilgrimage to visit a Christian healer trumping the other two. Was I a hypocrite? Could someone of my former faith really hold the answers for me? I had read about people who had given up their former lives because they had been "touched by God." Would I be that lucky to be chosen for that experience? Maybe my Joan of Arc fantasy would be realized. Or, worse, what if I went and felt nothing? I tortured myself with questions and, I am sure, tortured Mike as well. I was at a serious spiritual crossroads.

I had the feeling that any sliver of spirituality I had was slipping away. I wanted my life to be a whole entity that would encompass a deeper understanding of the world on a spiritual level. I yearned for life to be simple where I could hear myself breathe and feel my heart beat. I wanted to be connected to something greater than I was. I began feeling hopeful that I would have a spiritual awakening with John of God, if I could somehow just get down there.

The fantasies continued. I wondered what it would be like to be one of the pilgrims that flocked to John of God's side. I was intrigued at the deepest level about the blind faith and conviction that made their lives look so much easier than my own. My fear that God was really Catholic and I had totally screwed myself by converting would be over. I could just follow and not think. It would all be part of God's plan.

ه

Regardless of how I dissected this fantasy trip, none of it really mattered towards the end. The lives of my family members evolved to a new normal, peppered with cancer setbacks and emotional hurdles. As my mom squeaked into September of 2009, the increasingly difficult task of making it through the day pushed any trips to healers in far-off lands further into the realm of the unrealized. Team Nancy's days were riddled with bullet holes created by the ever-present conversations about my mom's frightening condition. As local healers promised "relief" and asked for more money, our family had more realistic conversations about my mom dying.

As we were gearing up to have painful discussions about hospice, hope arrived in the most interesting fashion.

One bright day in September of 2009, in the healing light of my mother's closet, I was trying on a striking, newly delivered pair of Oscar de la Renta black silk heels with oxblood gems and feathers as my mother was asking questions about the new garden project I was planning to install at the charity she had founded. It made her laugh as I twisted my ankle turning on the carpet. She wondered outloud how I would look in the garden in those shoes, teaching worm composting to teens aged out of the foster care system. My mom had become tired, really looking worn out. I was trying to keep the conversation light when the phone rang. Rita buzzed on the intercom to say Krishna, Bobby's wife, was on the phone.

It was a short conversation, but my tired mom went from weary to purposeful as she grabbed a pen to write down details.

"What is it?" I asked.

"You're not going to believe this! Guess who is going to be in New York in three weeks!" she shouted with the joy of hearing the best news possible.

I couldn't begin to think of who could get my mother that excited.

"Krishna just told me John of God is visiting the Omega Center in Rhinebeck, New York!"

I am fairly sure the glee on my face matched my mom's. I smiled as big as I could, first thinking my mom could finally meet him, and then thinking about my own possible salvation.

Weak no more, my mom once again had purpose. As she started ripping through her closet, my mom gave Rita the list of things she needed to prepare for the trip. Rita looked at me with hopeful yet concerned eyes. The message between us was clear and simple: It was time to get Mama to New York.

II.

PILGRIMAGE

| CHAPTER FIVE |

The cancer had spread to her peritoneum, causing her CAT scans to look like intense constellations. The cancer was also sneaking into her lungs, causing them to fill with fluid. Breathing became harder and my mom was fearful she would die a slow and painful death by drowning. The waste produced by the cancer cells was manufacturing so much fluid that it also put pressure on her organs. As a result, she was in constant pain.

The month leading up to our trip was filled with such dire medical news, I wondered if it would ever become a reality. Our first priority was to keep Mom comfortable. For this, her doctors suggested a thoracentesis, the draining of the lung with a catheter to alleviate the pressure and increase her ability to breathe.

It was a simple procedure that involved a needle to be inserted into the area surrounding her lung. The person recommended was at UCLA, so Rita scheduled the first of what would be three of these procedures. Since I was the one who could best handle these sorts of things, I volunteered to go. I was happy to spend the time with my mom, but I also wanted to witness the procedure and get an idea from the doctor how advanced my mom's cancer was.

The morning of the procedure, my anxious mom took more than her share of pain meds. She was anxious in the waiting room but decided not to take any more pain medicine until she was called into the room. I escorted her down the hall and helped get her undressed.

She had developed a habit of apologizing to me for seeing her in such a state. I fought back tears and told her she was still as beautiful as she had always been.

She slipped her arms into the oversized hospital gown and handed me her clothing to fold and put into her bag. Here was once again the delicate balance: wanting to keep things light and yet wanting to pay attention to the serious things going on around me. The tightrope I had been walking for the last few years became longer every time I had to figure out how to show the right amount of concern and emotion without getting teary.

My mom wouldn't allow me to be with her if I was emotional. She didn't want to upset me but also didn't want to deal with my emotions. She wasn't in any frame of mind to be concerned about any of our feelings anymore. So when she would say things to me like, "I am sorry you have to see me looking this way," I could never look her in the eye. In fact we had stopped making eye contact months before. It was just too hard. If she were able to look me in the eye, she would see how sad and afraid I really was. Perhaps I would have seen the same in her shoes, and that was something I was not willing to deal with. When we were together, she and I were still in Barbie Land. Dealing with the real emotions was just too difficult.

The doctor came in, breaking the silent trance we had fallen into. The wait had stretched into a half hour. He asked my mom how she felt, and when she responded, "Anxious and a little nervous," he invited her to have more pain medicine. I was slowly shaking my head, hoping he would see that I was trying to tell him she had already had enough, but he didn't catch on. I didn't think she was about to overdose, but I wasn't sure how much would be too much.

He instructed her to sit on the side of the bed, facing me. He put a pillow on the portable bedside table and told her to rest her arms on that. I could hold her hands as the procedure took place. So as she faced me, her gown undone, the doctor started to explain what was going to happen. First, he swabbed the left side of her back with iodine. Her head started to nod forward as the last dose of pain medicine coursed though her veins. In fact, she got herself so dosed up, she fell asleep during the procedure and had no recollection of it at all. Once it was clear she had nodded off, I had the job of keeping her up straight so she didn't fall over and possibly have the needle he was about to insert puncture her lung. I was amazed at how hard it was to keep such a tiny lady from falling over.

I took the opportunity to talk to the doctor about this procedure and what it ultimately meant. He explained that since the cancer had spread to her lungs, this procedure would be something she could do on a regular basis, until she decided she no longer wanted any more intervention. Again, the allusion of hospice was hanging over us. I drifted back and forth between blinding reality and comforting Barbie World throughout the conversation, not sure where I would feel more secure. I asked him how others dealt with this procedure, and he said he had one woman who came in monthly, hiked up her shirt, bent over the bed, and toughed it out. She scheduled it before she went and played cards with her girlfriends. I had a hard time believing my mom would incorporate this into her schedule. With the simple mention of "not wanting any more intervention," I wasn't sure how long she would even be around.

The doctor and I made small talk as he continued draining her lung. I watched as a one-liter bottle filled with fluid. I asked him if this was common, since it was hard to believe my mother's body was holding on to that much liquid. I asked about its color and consistency too, hoping they were like tea leaves in the bottom of a glass and could predict my mom's future. The fluid was a little sludgy, the color of bile. To the doctor, this was not nearly as bad as seeing dark fluid, which meant blood and more cancer than my mother had.

The entire procedure took less than an hour. As he was finishing up, and my arms were getting sore from trying to keep my mother from leaning over, the doctor explained that her comfort should be better, but there was no telling for how long. He recommended we come back in a month to do another one. If she had been awake, she never would have done this again. But seeing that she fell asleep during the procedure, I reconsidered the possibility of it being a monthly thing.

Having discussed with my brothers and the rest of Team Nancy the procedure and how my mom slept through the whole thing because of her overzealous attention to pain medication, we ended up convincing her to make a visit to a pain management specialist. It wasn't just this latest procedure; it was an accumulation of months of her managing her own pain by popping whatever pills she wanted. One of the side effects from the morphine was constipation and stomach cramps. In the spirit of keeping the family happy, and trying to find her own balance for her compromised digestive system, my mother capitulated and went with a program of less medication to manage her pain.

Bobby took her to this appointment. The pain doctor gave her a manageable regimen my mom said she would follow. Over the next week, my mom started to perk up. She was more aware of what was going on, and for a little bit of time I thought I was getting my old mother back. Unfortunately, I couldn't talk to her about the change in her behavior, because it would have been seen as critical of how she had been before. Instead, I called a little more and shared more information about the kids. She was slightly more energetic, but still not interested in eating. It seemed like this new plan would be a good one. But her coughing had returned and it was time to schedule another thoracentesis.

In hindsight, pain management had not been the best idea.

My mom showed up to UCLA with clear eyes and her crosswords. She was acutely aware of her surroundings, with no idea what the thoracentesis was going to feel like. She had only been slightly aware when the previous one had begun. As far as I knew, any pain with this procedure would be from the insertion of the needle. I didn't think anything would hurt after that. So we went through the same motions as before, had the same doctor come in and explain what was going to happen. My mom was a trooper, though, and said that she was anxious and nervous but thought she would be all right. He swabbed the same area again as she prepared herself for the needle. I gripped her hands as the doctor counted to three. This time, though, the size of the needle was a little more than my mother could bear. She shouted in pain. She looked at me with hurtful eyes.

Was this my fault? I was the greatest advocate for pain management. Was my mom cutting back on her meds for my sake?

I felt terrible. Even if it wasn't my fault, I had terrible guilt to the point where I got her morphine out of her bag, ripped open the pouch, and gave her whatever she wanted.

I wanted to cry but, knowing the ground rules, decided to look her in the eye and tell her that she was going to be all right. I put everything I was feeling aside so we could both make it through the rest of the procedure.

She started to relax as the morphine took effect. Her grip on my hands lightened ever so much, indicating she was drifting off. Again, I held her hands as she sat across from me, holding her up as she started to nod off a bit. He allowed us to stay in the room until my mom woke up enough to walk out on her own. It may have been less than an hour as I watched my mom resting. Her eyelids fluttered with the rhythm of her dreams. It was a rare, peaceful moment watching over her, finally able to protect her from the evils of cancer.

Grateful that Tim had driven Mom to the hospital, I rushed to my car after I had said a lighthearted goodbye and congratulated my mom on completing another painful procedure. The valet at UCLA was quick. For that, I was grateful. I knew I had the strength to see my mom through anything she had coming. I knew I could suck in all my emotions and not think about anything until I was done. But the letdown afterwards, and my ability to recover from it, was getting more difficult. I got in my car and headed out from underground. The Los Angeles light was harsh as I signaled to make a right to get myself home.

Pulling over, I realized I was on the verge of a panic attack. The signs of a big one were coming at full force. Tunnel vision, shallow breath, and the urge to jump out of the car and run as fast as I could. I turned on the air-conditioning as high as I could and blasted it right at my face. I turned on some classical music and laid my hands palms up on top of my thighs. Closing my eyes, I started to breathe deep, counting to five on the inhale and then to ten on the exhale.

No thoughts, just my breath. I could have sat there for hours, pretending nothing else existed. Then came the tears.

What was it that I needed? Other than for my mom to wake up healthy, what was it that I needed to calm my soul? What was it any of us needed?

Wine wasn't helping; neither was chocolate, potato chips, or french fries. I was losing every bit of control and realized every waking moment was filled with the fear of losing her. I had no strength to talk to anyone about how I was feeling. I was afraid of even mentioning the words "What if she dies?" The sadness was welling up from depths I didn't even know I had. How could watching my mother disintegrate be so physically painful? How could the love I had for her be so challenged? If I weren't so devoted, I would have made myself less available. But I chose to be there for everything I possibly could. I chose to play the role I was playing and chose to be the strong one so I could oversee what was happening. I was angry I had decided to be so strong. Maybe if I had been less available I wouldn't hurt as much as I did. I wanted to stop time, stay in the car with the cold air on my face, and just breathe. Nothing, here, could hurt me.

Our departure date was rapidly approaching. The excitement was building, but we had one more thoracentesis to do so my mom could be comfortable on the plane. Her cough was consistently building during the two weeks since her last one. But based on the last two experiences, we felt safe in scheduling the appointment for the Friday before we left. It was advised we do the treatment as close to departure time as possible so there would be no extra pressure on her organs. I went to the bad place of picturing her lung blowing up on the plane and having to make an emergency landing as my mother dramatically bled out next to me.

We arrived once again at UCLA at 7:30 AM and waited over an hour. The doctor we had both times before was not there, even though we had confirmed he would once again do the procedure. A doctor unfamiliar to us was scheduled but was not yet in the building. I should have recognized this as a red flag to get us out of there. But we were so on the track to get my mom to New York, to John of God, that we stuck with the plan.

My mom's nurse, Tim, and I were there this time because I had made a last-minute hair appointment before our trip, and I didn't want to leave her alone there. We were all a little agitated from waiting so long and nervous the procedure wouldn't be performed by the doctor my mom had begun to trust. She was also much less medicated, so she was very aware of what was happening, although equally determined to just get this one over with.

I was feeling silly that I had a hair appointment when there was a possible catastrophe brewing. But when I told my mom I would cancel the appointment to stay with her, she repeated her favorite line loud enough for the reception nurse to hear: "I have cancer. Do your old dying mom a favor and color your hair." It was the only time in my mother's illness that she (a) said the word "dying" and (b) pulled the cancer card on me. I had a few grey hairs coming in and wasn't really bothered by it. I was actually fascinated with how I was aging. As long as my reflection in the mirror was less Maleficent and more Sleeping Beauty, I was willing to let the grey go. However, at the sight of the first five of my grey hairs, my mother was appalled. The conversation went something like this:

MOM: Dear Jesus, what is going on with your hair!

ME: Huh? What do you mean?

MOM: There's grey in there! I am too young to have a daughter with grey hair!

ME: Mom, you're ridiculous—who cares what color my hair is? No one cares, and it's not that bad.

MOM: Please go get your hair colored—I will pay for it!

ME: Mom, I can pay for my own hair color and no thank you. I don't want to color my hair.

MOM: Ugh, fine. But you should color your hair. It won't take long—just do it. Please. Please go get your hair colored!

So here we were, at UCLA, with me about to leave for a hair appointment so I wouldn't embarrass her anymore. It was a running joke but had a tone of seriousness to it. My mom had become concerned that I was letting myself go because I was spending too much time taking care of her. If I colored my hair, I would be, during that short amount of time, paying attention to myself rather than her.

I hated leaving but realized as I rushed to the car that I was incredibly relieved when she gave me the out. I was afraid if I stayed it would be like the last time, with me pulling over doing my best to avoid a panic attack. I was afraid the procedure would be worse because the new doctor didn't know my mother. I felt overprotective, as if nothing would be right if I was not present. As I waited to exit the parking lot, I actually paused to reconsider the day's itinerary. Do I pull over and cry? Do I cash out my bank account and drive to Mexico, call Mike and tell him to get the kids from school and come join me so we can open a taco stand on the beach? It seemed reasonable to me at the time. My next question was way more rational: Which bars opened at 8:00 am? I figured something around Skid Row but didn't want to hassle with parking downtown. How about cake? Could I make it to SusieCakes in Brentwood before my appointment, and would it be OK to eat a huge slab of chocolate cake with dye in my hair? I was looking for anything to escape the pressure of the position I had put myself in. I watched people passing before my car as I waited for the light to turn green. Students on their way to class, smiling and laughing with their friends, had no idea what was happening inside my car. There was a whole world outside of my mother's cancer that I was missing because I was in so deep I couldn't see what was around me anymore.

I had divided my life into roles. I was the happy mom when my kids came home from school. I was the good wife when Mike came home. I was the doting daughter making sure my mom was comfortable. There was no room left for anything else.

Everything in my life had boiled down to these three tracks I traveled on daily. I had allowed her cancer to rule my life. I don't know when it happened, when that turning point was, when I had become consumed by the cancer, but I was so deep in it I didn't know how to escape. These fantasies I had in the few seconds it took to drive the car up the ramp to the street were the first escapist fantasies I had during the years of my mom's illness. What if I did just up and leave? What if I took a "mental health year" and just disappeared? Would I save myself the grief of watching my mom shrivel away into nothing?

As I entertained each scenario and flushed them out with incredible details, I miraculously made it to my hair appointment. I sat in the chair without speaking, fearful if I had to answer the simple question of "How are you?" I would slide onto the floor and melt in a pool of unstoppable tears. I turned my phone off and slipped it into my bag, determined the next two hours would be silent ones. I read gossip magazines, caught up on the lives of stars I had never heard of, and felt my shoulders slide back down into a restful position. Maybe my mom was right. Maybe a dye job would be just enough to get me off the tracks I had been on and onto one where I actually mattered.

My temporary reverie was shattered once I got in the car and turned my phone back on. I had six messages from Tim, my brothers, and Rita. I came to find out that my mother's experience was terrible and painful. She had to wait another half hour before she saw the doctor, who turned out to be arrogant and rude. Even though he was filling in for our trusted doctor, he had not performed a thoracentesis in a number of years. Regardless, he insisted on moving ahead as he jabbed my mother with the needle. I was horrified and filled with guilt, since I was sure I would be to blame for this. It had to have been my fault, since I had left for something so superficial. My mom had medicated herself so much that she was incapable of speaking coherently. Tim had to carry her into the house and put her in bed. She was speaking nonsense when my brothers and I met at my mother's house later that day. She remembered she had been at the hospital but didn't remember any details. As far as we were concerned, that was not a bad thing.

Looking back on it, if I had been there, would it have made a difference? I was not sure how I felt about this. Did I feel guilty for leaving and allowing this to happen, or did I feel self-righteous that nothing could be done properly without me? I'd like to think that I would have saved the day and prevented the doctor from going further once my mom's pain got so severe she cried. But if I had intervened, it would have changed the course of events that lay ahead. My decision, my absence from the room, was the pivotal moment that steered our sinking ship in another direction.

_ن_

The House of Cancer that Friday was filled with exhaustion and sadness. My mom was with us only in body. Her tiny frame could not handle the pain medication, so she lost track of what she was saying. It was a challenge to keep up with her lines of conversation, since her health was dramatically declining. It had happened before. But we were all so tired, it was hard not to cry when she began talking about a board meeting with a total stranger after being asked how her pain was.

The energy we all had to muster up to have conversations with the doctor was increasingly difficult. I wished we could have had these conversations in repose. Maybe warm beverages could be in our hands, with us wrapped in blankets to shield us from the constant incoming mental exhaustion we faced around the clock. I wanted to close my eyes and escape the mounting anguish we were feeling as September was coming to a close. I was tired of crying, tired of separating my emotions, and tired of the constant drama that surrounded my mother. However, my wishes were not granted as my brothers and I filed into the kitchen with the doctor and my mother, grabbing bottles of water as we all sat around the kitchen table, making decisions on how we would move forward from here on out.

Obviously, given the day's events, none of us wanted Nancy to fly to New York. The whole thing was becoming absurd given her rapid decline. But now in her seriously compromised state, it was seemingly impossible. Convincing her otherwise, though, was just as impossible. My mother was the strongest and most determined woman I knew. Even though she was still talking nonsense, she was one hundred percent focused on her goal of meeting John of God. She wanted this pilgrimage. Given her determination, it would be heartbreaking for us to tell her she was not allowed to travel. I think if we had done that, it would be time for her to give up. We were so sad for her, and for us, that we were willing to do anything to make her happy. She was alone, dying, and out of it most of the time. Everyone, including my dad and Carole, gave her as many outs as she needed.

But she was already packed. She was going with or without me.

The doctor laid out specific rules for the remaining days before the trip. My mother was not supposed to leave the house; she was to listen to the nurses and generally behave. She was going to have to sit with oxygen in her home since her lung was filling up more rapidly between treatments. She asked us if she was grounded. A close watch was kept on her so she would be all right to leave for New York. But since my mom was given a bright yellow caution sign accompanying her permission to travel, she felt like she had won. "No" was not in her vocabulary anymore.

I was secretly hoping the trip would get cancelled. When I thought about the enormity of my responsibility to her, I became terrified. I was supposed to be boarding a plane with her alone, tending to her every need, making sure she didn't try to walk in the airports, watching to make sure she didn't wander off or leave things behind. Once I expressed my fears to Rita, my father, and Carole, it was decided that we would bring a nurse with us. I was simply not trained to travel with someone so ill. While my mother was optimistic I could take care of anything, I insisted that we bring someone with us. In fact, I made it a deal breaker. But in order to retain some control, she decided to pick the nurse for the trip.

As fate would have it, a new nurse had just been hired, someone who had just moved to L.A. from up north. She had been in the house for about a week before my mom decided she was the one to come on the trip. I was introduced to her one day while visiting my mom. Laurie seemed really nice on first impression. I noticed she had a few tattoos and looked like a nice surfer girl with a good story. She looked to be the same age as me and came across as professional and kind. When my mom told me Laurie was coming with us, I was just glad my mom had made a decision and chosen someone she liked the best. But my mom probably chose Laurie over the other, more scheduled nurses because Laurie knew the least about the family dynamic. I didn't care who it was. I wasn't looking to make a new friend; I was just happy I had some help.

My job on this trip was large. I was to be chauffeur, facilitator, schlepper, confidante, and peacemaker. I had to keep up the energy without pushing too much, gently suggest breaks when my mom looked tired, and do my best to stay serene so my mom could enjoy herself. Even for the magnitude of my role, I was infinitely relieved that I had Laurie there to manage my mom's health. The three-inch binder outlining her medication and care was more than I could handle.

There were a few more obstacles causing me anxiety. First, I was extremely uncomfortable with the prospect of navigating LAX with my dying mother, even with Laurie there to help. Thankfully my mom agreed to a wheelchair, so at least I would have that assistance. She had balked at it at first, not wanting to appear in public like the invalid she was, so I told her it was for me. I said that I planned on drinking heavily on the plane, so she would need to wheel me off and get me to the rental place so I could drunk-drive her to Rhinebeck. My own need to self-medicate was great. However, drinking was less of an option, since I was aging less gracefully than I had planned and was getting hangovers from two glasses of wine. I was a disgrace to my Irish roots.

Second, I was really nervous about flying with her, since my mom was so susceptible to others' illnesses. What if she caught a cold, or worse, what if she died in flight? Would I even let anyone know or just cover her with a blanket and wait to land? I am sure there's protocol for that, but I didn't want to learn it. I was also strangely self-conscious about traveling with someone so sick. She was bone thin, didn't eat anything, coughed up gross things in tissues all the time, and often said odd things. She tried to look tranquil, but her smile always revealed how much pain she endured. I had gotten used to it, but how would a passenger on the plane feel about traveling next to a dying woman? I know sitting next to someone on a plane who sneezes makes me wish I had traveled with hand sanitizer and a particle mask. Would I have to explain that my mother's gurgling coughs were not from anything contagious, or could I just cast a knowing look to watchful passengers and pretend I didn't know her? Or should I just disclose in hushed tones to those closest to us that she had the c-word? Even worse, what if I was next to someone who would give me a wink and tell me their own parent cancer story? I didn't want to discuss the reasons for dragging my dying mother across the country. Isolation was much preferred when I started to think about it.

Lastly, when I thought about the logistics on the other side of the country, I got anxious. I didn't have any trouble playing cruise director for any other trip, but this one needed extra time built in to make sure we got to our destinations on time. I had to plan for emergencies. The itinerary had us taking a late-morning flight to JFK from LAX. We were to stay in a hotel close to the airport, and the next morning, I would rent a car, pack us up, and drive to Rhinebeck. Normally playing cruise director appealed to my interest in retaining some control over activities. But this time, I had convinced myself I was not capable of handling anything. I started to identify where the closest hospitals were, where the nearest clean bathrooms were, where the mini-marts were, and what the best travel times were so we could make it there without traffic. The list of what-ifs went from silly things like, would there be gluten-free food for me, to what if I got lost coming back to the hotel from the car rental, to how would I deal with my mom dying in the hotel? I had not driven the highways in New York in years, so I had no idea how to get from Long Island to Rhinebeck. I was not keen on the navigation system either, since my dyslexic brain never quite understood where to make the next left. As a result, I ended up making far too many legal U-turns. I had spiraled down into a ridiculous self-deprecating quagmire.

I decided the person to talk me off my ledge was Carole. She was as even as could be, calm and resourceful. I hoped that she would take mercy on me and offer my dad's plane. If this was the case, my mom could rest comfortably the whole time. No one would look at us sideways, and she could cough as often as she wanted. My stress would be reduced exponentially, since I would not have to guide my mom and all her stuff through an airport.

Why I didn't come right out and ask for this favor was really idiotic. This was not my usual mode of transportation, so initially it did not even occur to me to ask. But it was the way my dad traveled. He had worked extremely hard since he was twelve years old and found himself in a position to own his own plane. But I wasn't one to ask for that sort of thing. Not that I was a martyr, but I never felt it was my place to ask for such a large favor. I have no doubt that my father would have said yes; he is more than generous to his family. But I have my dad's sense of pride and figured that when I got past all my craziness, I could actually do this on my own. Besides, I was raised to not run to Daddy every time I needed something. I'm pretty sure if the positions were reversed and I owned the plane, he would be just as hesitant to ask me. And I, of course, would do whatever was in my power to help him.

That's just who we are.

But, at the end of the day, I am practical. If he offered, I was not going to say no.

So when my dad actually did call and offer the plane, I nearly cried. Now the trip's level of difficulty had just decreased. I could get my mom on that plane, get her set up on a couch, and let her sleep comfortably the whole time.

More importantly, having that pressure dropped meant I could relax and focus on the reasons behind the trip.

| CHAPTER SIX |

What happens when Yom Kippur, John of God, and a dying mother come together at the same time? Sounds like the beginning of a really bad joke.

While the details of my mom's itinerary were being solidified, I was attempting to do some meager planning for myself. It was September, and Jews were entering the High Holidays, a serious time for reflection. It was the time of year for us to take stock of the year's activities and assess how well they had gone. It was an opportunity to reflect on how I could have done things better and a time to prune away negative feelings and regrets. Given my preoccupation with the metamorphosis of my spirituality, it was a perfect time for me to find a place to be pensive.

Yom Kippur, the Day of Atonement, was to fall on the Monday we arrived in Rhinebeck. Jewish holidays actually begin at sundown. The service that welcomed Yom Kippur morning would begin on Sunday night. If the timing was right, I was hoping the Sunday we were to arrive in Rhinebeck, I could find a temple where I could participate in my favorite service, Kol Nidre. This literally translates into "All Vows." It's actually a legal formula that releases people from vows we will make in the coming year. We ask God to wipe them out and forgive us for any transgressions. So for all the resolutions we won't hold on to, even though we swear to God this year is going to be different, we ask for forgiveness and God gives us the assurance that we'll be OK.

The service itself is the most beautiful one of the year. The prayer is recited three times, effectively asking God to release us. I needed that. The entire congregation stands as all the Torahs are removed from the ark. Together we renew our faith and pray for a better year. The cantor chants a haunting melody that invariably sends me into deep meditation. The prayers are followed by incredibly soulful music that allows me to escape even further into myself. At its conclusion, I am refreshed and ready to start a new year, perhaps a little more conscientiously than before.

I was hoping that a magical reconnection with my faith would occur if I were to observe in earnest on my favorite night of the Jewish calendar. I hoped in doing that with a bunch of strangers, it would be all the more meaningful. Being the unidentified woman in the back of the room would mean I wouldn't be the person in charge of the food pantry. I wouldn't be the poor woman with the dying mother. I wouldn't be the mother of two children and I wouldn't be the one living with conflict and sadness. I would be an anonymous congregant, wishing only to share a common experience with my fellow Jews. For a few hours, I could escape everything.

In whatever Kol Nidre service I could find, I was going to take my religion to therapy. If I was going to break up with Judaism, I had to give it a fair shake before I moved on. I wanted the space to think about what I wanted for myself. There were still so many things about my chosen religion that I truly loved, and I was willing to make the same list about how I had not committed enough. My initial attraction to being a Jew was that it was so different from my experience as a Catholic, where we had to take the Bible at face value. There was no questioning; it was just acceptance. Since I was never willing to just accept anything without myriad questions, being a Jew fit my personality. The Torah was filled with lessons that were applied differently every year. There was always room for debate; in fact it was encouraged.

My involvement in the Tikkun Olam committee, where we were charged with changing our area of the world, had me excited about being involved in the community. Our commitment to social justice and helping others wasn't a way for us to jump the velvet ropes in front of St. Peter. We helped others for the sake of doing just that. If we happened to feel better about ourselves while doing the right thing, then so be it. We were charged with making the world a better place for those who were less fortunate. There wasn't any hidden agenda; it was because it was the right thing to do.

Perhaps my Catholic upbringing had convinced me that there was only one way to be close to God, and that was simply by being an active member of my religion. I wasn't ready to give it up. If I could recapture my connection, then maybe I could once again find comfort in regular Friday-night services. Maybe I just wasn't trying hard enough. I still had not given up the black-and-white dilemma I had put myself in, that I had to be one religion and follow it. It would take a little while to understand that I could be whatever I wanted to be and still feel close to God. I felt like friends of mine on their second and equally unhappy marriages who wouldn't get a divorce because it was a sign of personal failure. Ditching my relationship with my religion because it wasn't quite working for me at the moment would make me feel like a flake. Perhaps as well, it was my need to control something in my life.

With the help of Rabbi Stein, I found a congregation close to the hotel. Now I just had to hope I could make it there in time. I mentioned to my mom my plan to go to temple. She shrugged and smiled. She told me that I should do whatever I wanted, now that Laurie was coming with us. I didn't go into specifics with her as to why I wanted to go—I knew this was not a conversation she would be interested in having. My spiritual dilemma would have been looked at as a waste of time. My mom didn't think in those terms on a good day, and I know she was not interested in indulging me in my angst as she was coughing up discolored fluid from her lungs. I knew she would ask me why I was making such a big deal about this, and I would not have an answer. I wasn't really certain. However, finding a temple was a good start for me. Finally feeling that clarity lay ahead, my spirits were picking up. The promise of hope and a fresh start were waiting for me in Rhinebeck. I was certain.

I left my house that morning finally feeling like this trip was going to be well worth it. It would be good for my mom to have her last hurrah and good for me to attend to my spiritual needs. I didn't want to burden Mike with these issues anymore.

My patient, loving husband always listened to me and, when needed, had the right words too. He took care of me better than anyone ever had. My relationship with him was able to go so deep because I had been in such despair. My defenses were down, so I laid everything out in front of him, and he scooped me up with the same unconditional love my mom had given me. I depended on him so deeply, finally finding the safest place I could be. His calmness made me breathe easier. When I needed a place to turn, he was always there for me. I wished he could have come with us, so I could snuggle in at night. With my strength renewed from a restful night's sleep with my husband, I would be able to face whatever day lay ahead in Rhinebeck. His birthday was a week away, so I planned on doing something really special when I came back. I wanted to thank my fantastic husband for providing a padded room where I could safely spin out of control.

I gave Mike a big hug and kiss before I left, excited that I would come back a lighter and changed person. As I closed my car door, I promised to call when we landed. Driving to my mom's at that time on a Sunday took enough time for one song, so I put on one of my favorite songs by Paul McCartney, "Maybe I'm Amazed." I figured blasting this declaration of love and dedication would float me all the way to New York as a strong and focused woman.

Cheerfully, I arrived Sunday morning at my mom's house to find my skinny mother still throwing things into bags. As she was putting things in, Tim was taking them out. Later I would thank him for his ability to edit her belongings. After all was said and done, I had one bag, and she had four. The suitcase bulging at the zipper was the one with her clothing. It was so big she could have fit in it, along with my two kids. Another had all her medications, and there was also one for her oxygen. Yet another held shoes and personal items. Then she had her carry-ons holding her magazines, paperwork, and crossword puzzles. I am not sure why this one was necessary, since she never looked at anything in that bag. She did not have the attention span to do a crossword, and she had stopped reading the emails that Rita had thoughtfully printed out. We had to fit all of this into the back of the car with the wheelchair. Her large bag was so heavy it took Tim, Laurie, and me to lift it.

Since it was early on Sunday, we made it to the Van Nuys airport in less than twenty minutes. We joked on the way that it was a really good thing we were traveling on my father's plane. Managing all my mother's baggage was more than two of us could handle. However, I was in a good mood, forecasting a bright and meaningful trip. Once we boarded and the luggage was stowed, Laurie and I set my mom up on the plane's comfortable couch. We wrapped her in a cashmere blanket, buckled her in, and effortlessly took off. My mom was coughing a lot, but it didn't seem to be anything too out of the ordinary. Laurie kept a close watch, taking her temperature, checking her blood sugar, and administering the volumes of medications it took for my mom to make it through the next few hours. I took a picture of my mom snuggled in. She was so frail but sporting the most satisfied smile. She had proven to everyone that she could make this trip.

I also took a picture of my mom's luggage compared to mine, figuring this would be a funny email to send. Some things, no matter how rough the circumstances, just never change.

With my mom tucked in and intent upon sleeping the entire trip, it gave Laurie and me a chance to get to know each other. As the fates may have it, Laurie had moved from Santa Rosa because her church, Agape, had relocated to Los Angeles. Being the spiritual person she was, there was no way around not being in church on Sundays. She and her teenaged son moved to be with their community. In church one Sunday after her arrival, she struck up a conversation with the woman sitting next to her. They talked about jobs, and when Laurie's conversation partner found out she was a nurse, she recommended that Laurie call her good friend Kelly, who was the very person in charge of my mother's case. Two days later, Laurie was at my mother's house on rotation.

I completely envied Laurie's conviction. Her faith was unwavering. I wished I had that kind of mettle, but I didn't. As she was talking, I wondered if I was just going to be a wandering soul, never quite content. I wondered if I would always be this hard on myself and prayed for a miracle to take me out of the morass I had plunged into. Laurie was so clear on her love for her faith. She didn't question anything nearly as much as I did; she just moved forward with the faith that God had a plan for her no matter what she did.

I started to think that our trip may be more than just a last-ditch effort for my mother. Signs were popping up that this was going to be bigger than just her and me. I had no idea how many other people were going to flock to Rhinebeck, but I was certain that they were going to be a lot more like Laurie than like me. I was going to have to change my attitude before arriving in New York.

In order to better understand what I had to do, I rummaged through the candy drawer to see if anything would inspire me. Just to be on the safe side, I found some potato chips as well. Maybe the balance between salty and sweet would aid my need for inner balance.

While contemplating the true genius of M&M's and potato chips, I realized that my mother had made a brilliant decision to bring Laurie. I also realized my mom was completely unaware of how smart she had been. It was hard to say how much my mother was aware of at this time. The cancer was everywhere. She had coherent moments and then slid into her less coherent ones. We all guessed she had chosen Laurie to accompany us because she lacked knowledge about my mom. But, what she really did was choose the most spiritually prepared person for this trip. Both of us would need a guide through this bizarre journey. Laurie was it. Little did she know that her role would be more than dispenser of medications and taker of blood pressure.

Now I was convinced I could have someone to talk to about what was going on, so I sat across from Laurie and started asking her questions about cancer. On the off chance she was more connected to God than she was admitting, I asked her a few questions about what her experience was with cancer patients. Specifically, I wanted to know what she knew about patients at the end of their lives. I wanted her to lay out the rest of my mom's timeline for me. When I told her we were hoping my mom would make it through Thanksgiving, she looked at me like I was nuts. She recovered quickly, since it was clear I was surprised by how large her eyes became, and said every case was individual and there was no telling how long my mom would be around. She just might make it to the end of November.

I think it was then that I truly realized my mom's time was coming to a close. Sooner, rather than later. The person who had kept me connected to my community and to my family was going to leave. I was going to be left to figure out how to exist without her. I had credited my mom with every success I had ever had. I owed everything to her. My sadness at times was so overwhelming, I was looking for answers on as large of a scale as possible. I wanted Laurie to tell me how it was all going to unfold, so I could be a little prepared.

Not wanting to appear overly emotional, I closed that conversation with hopeful words. I told her how grateful I was to have her on the trip, now for deeper reasons than before. I told Laurie that I was glad it was her coming with us, because I thought she would get just as much out of this as we would. I did my best to have a peaceful look on my face as I turned back to the kitchen.

Evening descended as we landed in Rochester. It was a rainy, slick fall evening with the perfect chill in the air. Even though the noise from the plane was drowning out the sound of raindrops, I could tell that once we were clear of the airport, we would be welcomed with the scent of wet leaves and the marvelous decay of nature preparing for winter. The darkness was comforting, masking a surge of anxiety that went from my belly to the top of my head. With my eyes closed, I stood in the rain for a few seconds, letting the anxiety radiate out through my fingers. The cool, moist air instantly calmed me, filling my lungs as I took one deep breath after another. I walked to the terminal with the pilot and got the keys to the rental car. I was pleased with how I was handling myself, since my exterior showed a completely calm and in-control grown-up. Nothing would have made me happier if I could be the child I wanted to be and have my mom take care of everything. Our role reversal had never been more pronounced.

By the time my mother got off the plane, all the bags were in the car. We were driving an extra-large SUV, so she needed a little help getting in. She had slept most of the way and was feeling rather chipper. Her eyes were bright and focused, ready for what lay ahead.

Once we were on the parkway, my mom started to talk to Laurie about me as if I weren't there. She chose this time to be oddly complimentary about my driving. She talked about the time I was following a car and driver in Rome one summer and managed to drive the streets of Rome like I was a resident. She talked about my expert driving in France, in Los Angeles, New York, D.C., and Arizona. It was an unusual conversation, since my mom wasn't really known for doling out lots of praise in our presence. We heard about how proud she was of us, or she would tell me that she had told someone how proud she was of my accomplishments, but I could not remember my mom praising me in front of someone else. It was almost uncomfortable.

"I feel so calm with my daughter around," she said.

I wish I could say this didn't faze me, but it did. I would have preferred to be angry or embarrassed. Instead, I was sad. Why had it taken this long for words like that to come out about me? I was tired and oversensitive at this point, but her praise felt awkward and undeserved. I could have said something like, "Calm on the outside, messy on the inside," but anything other than "Thanks, Mom" would have meant questions and tears. I had to get us to Rhinebeck and didn't want to take the time to pull over, sob, and explain why I was in such turmoil. Deep breaths, I thought—just keep breathing and I'll make it through.

"I just feel better when she's around. She just knows everything. She will get us there safely."

My mom slipped into her own thoughts as I started to pay more attention to the road. Like my mother said, I was an excellent driver. But there's nothing like driving unknown roads on a rainy evening. Always one to reflect on the deeper meaning of things, I thought of where we were, the time of year, and what was happening inside my mother's body. It was all so perfect, like it was scripted out for us. I knew this road would take us to our destination, but what would be there when we arrived?

We arrived safely at the Beekman Arms on the very late side of the evening. Nothing in town was open. The only person in the hotel was the night manager, who gave us our keys and sleepily informed us that the room my mother had reserved was not available until the following day. To most people this would have been a slight disruption that would be handled in the morning. But in our case, it complicated things at a near catastrophic level. I am sure I displayed a little more panic than I had intended as I explained our situation. It was of utmost importance, I told him, that everything at the hotel run smoothly. I started to laugh at myself as I told him about what we had in store for the week. I pleaded with him to make sure any transition would be a smooth one, since I couldn't handle any surprises. Since I had walked in with a frighteningly ill woman and spilled my guts out on the reception desk, the man took mercy on me and said they would accommodate our schedule and even move my mom's luggage to the new room once it was ready. OK, cross that off the list, I thought.

My mother was supposed to have a two-bedroom suite so she could spread out and Laurie could have her own space. Instead, they were in one room with Laurie on a pullout couch. I knew Laurie was aware of my mother's late-night activities, but I wasn't sure if she had actually witnessed them before. I was nervous thinking about it. I know Laurie was used to just about anything with her patients, so anything my mom would do at

3:00 AM probably wouldn't faze her. But I was concerned that my mom's facade of health and happiness would come down in ways that would embarrass her in front of Laurie. Sharing a room would mean that Laurie would see my mom as clearly as we did. I was certain my mom was not going to be happy about that.

I asked Laurie if she wanted to stay in my room and I would be with my mom for the night. I knew I would not sleep anyhow, so I may as well let my mom get some rest without having to keep up appearances. Laurie put her hand on my shoulder and said, "I am here to take care of your mom; I am not here on vacation. I am working, so I will stay with her. Don't worry."

On that note, I left them. I took the car to my room, which was down the street and around the corner.

As I found a place to park I looked up to see the skies clearing. Clear skies meant everything would be that much easier: The wheelchair wouldn't get stuck in the uneven sidewalks, the white clothing we were supposed to wear for this pilgrimage would be less dirty, and driving would be a breeze. Apparently the Entities could enter our souls better if we were dressed only in white.

I looked at the clock, realizing it was so much later than I had imagined. I had missed any chance of meditating through Kol Nidre. Strangely, for all the pressure I had put upon myself, I was all right with not going. My exhaustion gave me enough clarity to tell myself that everything would work out as it was supposed to. I lugged my bag into the room and collapsed on the bed. I called home to report a successful first leg of the trip, found out what Mike's day had been like, and told him how I wished he had been able to come. "I would have no place there.

This is your trip with your mom," he said. "Who knows, it might be an adventure of a lifetime."

"Sure," I said, "it absolutely could be."

On that, we hung up. I got into bed wondering what the next day would bring.

| CHAPTER SEVEN |

The first day of any of my adventures consistently held three things: excitement to see something I'd never seen before, a little fear of not knowing what to expect, and a cynical anxiety that the whole thing would completely fail to meet expectations. I often thought if I dropped all expectations, I couldn't be that disappointed.

As I showered, I pictured a very dramatic scene at the Omega Institute—with lepers on crutches and dying cancer patients. I saw afflicted people moaning with bandaged appendages looking for holy water from Lourdes. Everyone was wandering in and out of billowing tents, searching for cures. Of course all of them would spring back to life after being touched by John of God. When it was my mom's turn for her blessing, John of God would put his hand on her head.

The Entities would zip in and out of her like she was on the Haunted Mansion ride at Disneyland. Taking turns passing through her, they would bring out more and more of the cancer. I could watch her face fill out to her former beautiful self, and she would turn to hug me for being the chosen one to witness such a miraculous event.

Now that was a miracle I was ready to witness. However, as I toweled myself off in that cold bathroom, I shivered knowing none of it would happen. For as much as I wanted a storybook ending, I knew my sick mama was approaching the end of her life.

My expectations lowered, I dressed myself in the required whites, hoping anyone who saw me in town would think I was only a nurse, instead of one of those weirdoes going to see that Brazilian guy. We had planned on getting there an hour and a half before the first session started, to check in, get settled, and get some breakfast. Ever food obsessed, I was curious what would be served. I assumed we would be going to a real touchy-feely place with lots of incense—perhaps there would be vegan fare? That would be fine by me, as long as any tofu scramble was accompanied by some gluten-free snacks. I didn't want to feel hungry while I was there. My preoccupation with food annoyed me, so I did my best to think about positive things, like the peace I was hoping to feel when I sat with others seeking cures of their own, there in the presence of a faith healer.

The skies had cleared, but it was still wet outside. My white sweats were dragging on the ground. I hadn't bothered to try them on before I bought them. I also hadn't brought any scissors to trim the hem. I checked myself out in the mirror. I was in white head-to-toe, except for my black clogs, feeling extremely self-conscious. White was never my color of choice. I gravitated towards warmer colors that masked any bulges or imperfections. I tugged at my top, sneered at myself, and re-signed myself to the anxiety growing in my gut. As I stared into my own eyes, I told myself that within an hour, I would be just another white-clad pilgrim. I would blend in with the others filing in to receive their blessings.

My room opened right out to the street. I felt like a beacon stepping out of the door onto the sidewalk. I kept my gaze down, afraid any eye contact would give away my growing in-security about what lay ahead. However, when I looked up, I saw a woman waiting at the bus stop on the corner, also dressed in white. Ah, another loony tune like us. I could tell my cyni-cism was kicking up a notch, as it usually did when I wanted to protect myself from any disappointment.

As I dug in my purse for my keys, I heard my mom up ahead of me, coughing. She was standing next to the car with Laurie, dressed in the most fantastic white outfit. She had on white jeans, a white turtleneck with a white V-neck cashmere pull-over, and a white denim jacket with a silver studded sunburst on the back. I had to shake my head and laugh. Of course my mom was going to be the best-dressed pilgrim! Just like with her surgery, if she looked this good, perhaps the Entities would be so moved as to match her insides to her outside.

I greeted Laurie, gave my mom a hug, and told her she looked fantastic as I helped her in the car. Laurie and I got the rest of her bags in the back with the wheelchair, chitchatting about how the night had gone. Laurie said my mom didn't sleep much but would talk to me about it when we had some privacy. She was very aware of how sensitive my mom was about us dis-cussing her like she wasn't present. I closed the back of the SUV, made it around to the driver's side, and climbed in. I asked my mom if she had slept well and she said she was rested and ready to go. I checked my rearview mirror and caught a glimpse of her sitting with her hands folded in her lap, looking happily out the window. She had shrunk so much at this point, she looked like a child waiting to go to a fair. Her face was brimming with anticipation. I asked her if she was ready as I programmed in the address for the Omega Center. She took as deep a breath as she could and said, "Yes! Let's get going!"

Driving through town, I spied a few shops I thought would be fun to peruse when we were back from our first healing. I made mental notes about what I would be looking for: trinkets for Leo and Julianna, birthday presents for Mike, and a sweater or wrap for myself. As soon as we left town, the beauty of the Hudson River valley unfolded in front of us. Leaves of every shade of red, yellow, and orange surrounded us. The previous night's storm had left leaves that carpeted the roads and swirled around the car as we blazed through. It was a sight to behold. I opened up my window to breathe in the clean, brisk morning air. It was an incredibly comforting smell—the freshness of rain, the slight decay of the organic matter on the ground, and that indescribable aroma of being in the middle of fall. It's one that makes me feel the need to spend as much time as possible outside, sunning my face, soaking up the last of the warmth before I get ready for winter.

The drive in total was about ten minutes. We went through the back roads of Rhinebeck, passing ponds, farms, fields, and a few farm animals. We made a right onto the street that would ultimately take us to the parking lot of the Omega Center. It was completely wooded, with sun-dappled birch surrounding us. There was a large pond on our left, no houses to be seen. I thought we must be lost. My mom must have slipped into the reverie too, since her face was towards the sun with her eyes closed. Laurie was doing the same. It was a sliver of a moment they were enjoying before whatever else lay ahead. They both had little smiles, revealing the relief they were feeling for having gotten this far.

I was hoping we were not lost, afraid of being late. Being late meant bad parking, maybe not getting a chance to eat breakfast, and possibly being singled out as the "late people" when we entered the tent, where all the attendees gathered for what I assumed would be the blessings of the day. Tardiness was one of my biggest fears. I hated being late for school when I was a kid, because I didn't want to be noticed for anything. I wanted to slip into my seat before the bell and blend in as much as possible. I never wanted any attention my way, because I was afraid the teachers would want an explanation. I was always so petrified of being called out in class, afraid I wouldn't have the right answer. Seemed so silly to be in my forties and feeling like I was in middle school, but that fear of being singled out never goes away.

Soon, we made our left into the parking lot of the Omega Center. I looked ahead, deep into the lot, trying to figure out the easiest access to the entrance, which looked to be to our right. It was hard to tell what the layout of the center was from the parking lot. All we could see from the inside of the car were lots of trees and the entrance building with a set of double doors that served as the main office and registration. Nothing was really marked, telling us where to go. We just assumed we would go through those doors and figure it out from there. The adventure was beginning.

The lot was not paved, and I could see that maneuvering the wheelchair was not going to be very easy based on the number of puddles I drove through. There was a parking attendant up to my left, so I poked my head out the window and smiled my biggest smile. I explained that I was with my mom who was in a wheelchair and we may need to leave early. I put my right hand on the rolled-down window for emphasis and lowered my voice. In a hushed tone, like I was giving away to the attendant a deep secret, I said she was really ill and there was just no telling how long we would be able to stay. As I was about to deliver my third and most dramatic sentence about her needing oxygen on top of being ill, the attendant undid the cord and directed us to park in the coveted close-to-the-entrance spot. I told my mom she would have to get in the wheelchair and play sick so the guy wouldn't make us move. She laughed, coughing between giggles to tell me that John of God was going to find out I had lied to the attendant for cherry parking.

"Ha ha ha, get in the chair and cough some more and look really sick as we go by the guy, Mom." She plopped in the chair, wrapped her blanket around her legs, put her oxygen in her nose, and we set off. Laurie hoisted the heavy bag with my mom's medication over her shoulder. I had my mom's purse and mine on the chair handles along with the oxygen. There was no denying our need for a little extra help as I attempted to wheel my mom through the pits and puddles in the lot. Oddly, we had yet to see anyone else in white. There weren't many cars yet, but we remarked on how strange it was that there was no one around.

We walked through the entrance and looked for the registration desk. It was a fairly blank canvas of a building: lots of interior space with very little adorning the walls, bathrooms and a registration desk to the rear and to the left of another set of double doors that led out to a walkway. There were red tile floors and off-white walls, like we were in a school that had not been kept up for some years. Everything was just a little dinged and a little stained. It wasn't exactly what I had envisioned. I had thought, based on how the event had been completely sold out, we would be entering a place with lots of signage and direction, perhaps some of those calming desktop fountains and some New Age music—something to ease you into a tranquil space. Maybe smiling people who could guide us to where we needed to go, or just someone to welcome us. I assumed since we were seeing this famous healer, there would be many others who would be needing assistance—at least if my arcane vision of Lourdes was to hold up.

It was slightly disconcerting that no one was around. We had been told people came from all over the country to see John of God, so we were a little confused as to why no one else was registering when we were.

I walked up to the desk and dug into my bag to find our papers. As I placed them all in front of the completely disinterested middle-aged woman in front of me, I smiled. I greeted her warmly, hoping she in turn would at least look at me. She took the papers, stamped them, handed me three wristbands, and told me what time the retreat started. I noticed she didn't give us wristbands from the prepaid breakfast pile, so I gently suggested to her that since we had paid for breakfast, we would need wristbands that said breakfast on them. She looked at me with frustration and placed three on the windowsill separating us. I glanced back at my mom, who was unaware of the silly drama unfolding in front of me. She was just cozy in her chair, ready to see what lay ahead. I was brusquely instructed to go through the doors ahead and wait for a golf cart that would take us up the hill to the tent. Flashing our breakfast wristbands, I asked if the cart could take us to the mess hall. Unfortunately, there was not a road up there, only a footpath. We would have to walk the rest of the way.

Great, I thought. The wheelchair was not one that was meant for anything other than touring a museum. It had small wheels with grey inflexible tires. It was fine to sit in, but it was one that had to be *pushed*. I looked up the hill to the mulch-covered trails zigzagging to the cafeteria. Ahead I could see pilgrims in white filing into the big main tent, congregating in smaller groups on the hill, or marching up the hill for food. It looked like an extremely organized ant colony. Onto the cart we went, with a chatty older guy who was fascinated with our being from California. The steering wheel was in one hand and the other held a paper cup filled with creamy coffee. His potbelly jumped with each bump, and I instinctively kept an eye out for my mother sitting behind me, hoping she wouldn't bounce right off. I asked him the easiest way to get a wheelchair up to the mess hall and he shook his head. "It's one thing we don't really have here, a wheelchair-accessible path. You're kind of on your own, unless your mom can walk a bit?"

There were a few white-clad pilgrims waiting for a ride down the hill when we came to a stop. I was hoping they would be patient as we got all the bags and wheelchair off the cart. To my surprise, no one helped us. I looked at them and smiled, but they were engrossed in their own conversation, edging closer to the cart as we were helping my mom off. I raised my eyebrows as one person slipped between my mom and the cart, not able to wait for us to get her into the wheelchair. My mom was completely oblivious, but I had already started my mental checklist of things wrong with this place. I thanked the guy who drove us, even though he sat in the cart while we struggled with my mom's gear. I had no idea if the Entities swirled around the place prior to the meeting to make a list of who needed the most work, so I thought any extra politeness might be noticed and brought to the attention of the One In Charge. Maybe exuding serenity would secure us a better position when it was our turn to go before the faith healer. Before we moved any further, to solidify my attempts at serenity, I asked my mom if we could take a picture in front of the statue that was in front of us. I thought it would be a decent one to send back to everyone. So Laurie snapped a quick one as my mom and I stood arms around each other, looking like we were tired yet happy to be there. My mom looked at it and wanted to know who the person was in the picture with us. I looked at her kind of funny and told her it was the statue. She looked at me like I was nuts and said, "Not the statue—I can see that. Who is the other person in the picture with us?" Laurie and I looked at each other like my mom was crazy, but I had a feeling she really had seen someone between us.

"I have no idea who that was, Mom." I said cautiously. My mom looked at it again and shook her head.

"I thought there was someone there with us." She said it blithely, waving her hand as she sat herself in the wheelchair. I slipped the rest of the bags onto the handles of the chair as Laurie tucked the blanket around her knees. While she and my mom chitchatted about what they thought they would see, I caught Laurie's eye and she nodded to me like she was going to tell me something when we had a moment alone.

But at that moment, whatever she had to say would have to wait. I was busy overanalyzing my increasingly negative thoughts as all my list of complaints grew in my head. I thought I had lowered my expectations enough that I would not be disappointed, yet there was something missing from this experience and I was having a hard time pinpointing exactly what it was. So far we had not seen one smiling person, no one had asked us if we needed any help, no one had shown any interest in us being there. I thought that was surprising. I think it was a safe assumption that seeing a famous healer meant we would be in a healing environment. Nothing that we had encountered thus far was remotely healing and warm. I was acutely aware of how little help was around, especially since people were coming from all over the country for this experience. Nothing was sitting right with me, but I had yet to figure out why.

In an attempt to resolve my inner conflict, I focused on getting my mom up the hill while she and Laurie talked about nothing in particular. I was hoping if the rest of the pre-show action improved I could erase any lingering negativity and really go with the flow of the day. So I braced myself behind the chair and began pushing my mom up the hill and onto the heavily mulched path to the mess hall. I was lost in my critique of what we had seen thus far and realized I was practically horizontal to the chair, using every ounce of strength to get it over each piece of bark on the ground. I was huffing loudly when my mom finally said she would get up and walk. I couldn't argue with her, but before I could ask to pull stuff off the chair so it wouldn't tip over, she stood up. The weight of what was on the handles caused the whole chair to tip back, almost dragging me down with it. It was a lovely little metaphor for how I was feeling about this experience. All the crap I was carrying was dragging me down. I had to find a way to let it go.

I picked up the things that had gotten tangled in the fall and followed my mom reluctantly up the hill. I left her chair outside, maybe kicking it just a little because it brought home exactly what I needed to do. I wasn't expecting some stupid wheelchair to be the beginning of my self-realization and, frankly, it was embarrassing. I was "supposed to" be experiencing a greater power that would intervene and make me feel whole. Regardless, kicking the chair was incredibly juvenile and wonderfully satisfying. Just to put a cap on my rebellious action, we went in through the exit. It was the closest door to us with the least number of stairs.

We entered a sea of white in a cafeteria filled with all the John of Godders. There was a lot of activity and a slight buzz of conversation, but it was oddly sedate. People were in little groups, chatting away, immune to what was happening around them. There were no glances up at the new people, no looks of welcome, and no effort made to make room for the woman who was clearly the most ill in the room. Everyone I saw looked incredibly healthy—no lepers, no crutches, no bandaged limbs, just really healthy people dressed in white. We were there at the tail end of breakfast, which I quickly noticed was far from vegan. Laurie and I found a table at the far end of the cafeteria and left my mom there. I got her some yogurt, sliced bananas, and a little egg, careful to give her enough of what she could eat and hopeful that the presence of extra food would encourage her to eat just a little more. The three of us sat there, wondering where the sick people were. I felt a little better knowing I was not alone in my vision of what the day could be. Since there was such a crowd in the cafeteria, we decided we should try to get to lunch a little early. It was going to be a logistical nightmare with the wheelchair and all the other pilgrims wanting to eat within the hour we had assigned for lunch. It was clear to us that we wouldn't be getting any help from anyone.

My mom managed to get down only half a banana and a few bites of yogurt. We gathered up our things and headed out the door. My mom decided to walk a bit, so the chair got loaded up with all our stuff. It was infinitely easier going downhill, until we reached the expansive grassy area where the tent had been erected. The rain from the night before had made it a swampy mess. Plywood boards had been laid down in a line so it was easier for people to get in and out of the tent. But even those would squirt mud as we rolled over them.

I was looking for some way to feel connected to this experience. The physical beauty of the place was comforting, but the people around us were so invested in their own experiences, I felt no connection to them at all. There were a few hippies there, Caucasian twentysomethings, stinky with dreadlocks, flitting about the entrance. They were barefoot with jingling anklets, muddy from the grass; the whole scene could have been a drug-free Grateful Dead concert. Seeing more familiar types made me feel a little more comfortable, since the crowd that lay ahead looked to be bottlenecking into the one entrance into the tent. I told my mom she had to get into the chair, and I would wheel her in. We were hoping there was a handicapped section so we could grab a decent seat.

The sun was out, there was a slight breeze, and the temperature was perfect. Even with Nature behaving harmoniously for this occasion, I was getting a little uncomfortable with the sheer number of people in front of us. There were more than a thousand pilgrims lining up to get into the massive tent. The closer we got, the more nervous I became. There was no handicapped entrance, and no one interested in helping a dying woman get close to seeing the last person she thought would give her some clarity and perhaps even a cure. I asked another potbellied man at the entrance where we could put my mom.

Again, no eye contact, just a sweep of his pudgy left hand towards the back of the tent. "Go back there."

I asked again, "Is there a place for wheelchairs though? So she can sit in it and see the stage?"

Without even looking at me, he responded, "No, just put it along the back and go sit. Don't block the aisle—it's a fire hazard." I huffed loudly enough that the guy gave me a look. Perhaps we should have gotten there earlier. This was a lot less organized than I had thought it was going to be. It was almost hostile, far from the comforting atmosphere I had anticipated. I was wondering if my chance for a spiritual healing was gone.

I was feeling more defensive and less open to change the more time I spent there.

I expected something enveloping and spa-like, a place where we would be helped to find a seat and made comfortable, and one that would allow me to feel open enough to shed the negativity and uncertainty I had about my spirituality. I was waiting for a sign, something that would indicate we were in the right place, that being here was absolutely correct. I would have settled for something minuscule, like a smile or a gesture from someone. But nothing came.

Upon entering the tent, I was smacked in the face with the smell of wet grass and a mass of humanity. It was eerily silent, so I felt compelled to whisper. There was a stage to my right, taking up most of what appeared to be the front of the tent. Someone was on stage, instructing everyone to be quiet as they found a seat, explaining the Entities were at work. Sure, I thought, maybe those Entities could work on everyone's mood. While they were at it, they could make it a little cooler inside the tent.

It was muggy inside, with moisture from the grass, too much carbon dioxide being exhaled, and not enough air circulation. My mom was perpetually cold, though, so this was a comfortable temperature for her. I figured once I got her settled in a chair, I would cool down enough to clear my head of all the black-hearted notions running through my mind.

With my mom's chair stowed, we filed over towards the far end of the tent where there were still rows of empty chairs. There were four sections of tightly packed rows of white folding chairs. They were zip-tied together so no one could move them. Each section had about forty rows, but each row was so long, it was hard to get to the middle. It was poorly laid out. Everyone else had packed into the front right of the tent, so the farther away we got from the crowd, the cooler it got. We moved into a row about halfway down the third aisle. We chose to sit on the end of the row, with my mom on the aisle in case we had to leave. She had a decent view of the stage for when the show started.

From up front, a tanned woman with a long braid, also dressed in white, told us to sit quietly with our eyes closed and breathe. The Entities would be at work helping John of God to figure out the blessings. It would be a matter of moments before he would come out and bless all of us.

Entities in my soul looking for the right blessing? This was not exactly the sign I was looking for.

All I could feel was how absurd this was turning out to be. People had come from all over to be in this man's presence. There was nothing happening on the stage, other than this woman repeating her directions. Perhaps a little music to get everyone in the right frame of mind would have been nice. An opening act would have been nice too. I was starting to give up on my turn for a spiritual cleansing, convincing myself that I was there just for my mother. I looked at Laurie, whose facial expressions showed me she was feeling the same way. Once we made eye contact, we started to giggle. Totally inappropriate, we knew, but it was a relief that we were both thinking the same thing.

There was a consistent murmur from the pilgrims as they settled in. I took the opportunity to quietly discuss with Laurie my thoughts about what I had experienced so far. When I started to talk about how little help we had received, she turned to me and said with wide eyes and a big smile, "I know! Isn't it weird that we're totally on our own? I just don't get it."

She had the same spa-like expectations that I had. I definitely felt better about my disappointment. Then we both launched into an exchange about the Entities. We both had questions like: How did these particular attendants know they were there at work? Were these people who came from Brazil and toured with him? Laurie really didn't know what to expect, so I told her about the psychic surgery videos I had seen and how it looked like only John of God knew when the Entities were around. Any video I'd seen showed lots of commotion and conversation, even clapping and dancing, not to mention smiles. If the Entities were real, why were they only effective when there was total silence? Did everyone under that tent really believe the Entities were figuring out all of our needs? Given our experience with the attendants thus far, and the atmosphere of the entire tent, there was nothing healing or spiritual about this. Laurie remarked that she felt nothing but the humidity while sitting there.

Attendants dressed in white were milling about the rows. None of them had peaceful expressions. They appeared to be looking to bust anyone talking, or doing something they shouldn't be. It felt a little like school, teachers keeping watchful eyes on their pupils, rulers in hand waiting to rap knuckles. As Laurie and I were finishing our private Q&A, a blond and angry-looking male attendant in a pair of snug white overalls moved swiftly towards us and put his finger to his lips. "Shhhh, the Entities are at work!" He pointed upwards, as if one of them were lingering above our heads. I was willing to admit that my judgment may have been clouded by my heightened expectations, but this public admonishing was enough. The absence of organization, warmth of spirit, and general kindness was confusing. How were we to be expected to just let the healing come with little more than the direction to be quiet? I really wanted to cool off and think. If I could excuse myself and take a walk in the woods I had seen as we trudged up the hill, I knew I would return with a better attitude.

There was no way I would do that to my mom, though; it was my job to stick with her and go along with what she wanted. So I closed my eyes and thought about what I wanted. My Joan of Arc experience was not going to materialize. I just didn't think I was open enough to really give every ounce of my being over to a higher power and just have faith that a spiritual life would unfold in front of me.

After the events of the morning, I thought more on the wheelchair incident and wanting to walk amongst the trees. One thing I was clear about: When I needed clarity, I needed to be outside. I required clean air, the silence that comes from the deep woods or a mountain trail. When I needed extra clarity, I got on my horse and we went to a hilltop and watched the Pacific Ocean's marine layer cascade over the Santa Monica Mountains and down into the valley below the ranch. But while I could sit for hours pondering what I supposedly needed, I remembered what was most important about this trip. I was here to share this experience with my mom. I was her guide. How I felt about how we were being treated should be secondary. I had to make sure my mom found here exactly what she wanted.

My needs could wait. I knew I had more time to figure things out. I looked to my left at my mom. She was so peaceful sitting with her eyes closed, covered in white blankets. We were told that the Entities could see through to your soul if you wore white, but with all those layers, I was not sure. She was really cute sitting there, tiny as could be. Her painful smile was relaxing. She was wide open, waiting for the miracle to start. I had brought her this far. Looking at her, I felt content. I had done what I was supposed to do. So I smiled, closed my eyes, and allowed whatever Entities were circling our section to dive right in.

While everyone was waiting with eyes closed, there were people on stage chanting something, saying John of God was moments away from stepping on stage. OK, I thought, opening my eyes. We had been in the tent for an hour, just sitting. From my vantage point, something was going on that the people on stage were trying to mask. I had no idea what it was, but it looked like something wasn't right. Any videos I had seen led me to believe that we would be listening to a little music, getting ready for the great arrival. But there was nothing to build our expectations. I looked at Laurie, who had her eyes wide open, scanning the crowd. She was no longer engaged either. She whispered that she thought John of God might not have arrived. Maybe he was late.

It was beginning to feel a little cult-like, as most everyone had kept their eyes closed. I looked at my mom, who was rummaging through her bag for a hard candy. It looked like even she was ready to move on. I asked her what she thought about sitting here for so long. She was a little dismayed that it wasn't that organized but figured they knew what they were doing. So she occupied herself with the contents of her bag. I started to look around the tent for signs that something was about to happen. All the aisle attendants had disappeared. The braided woman on stage walked off and the entire tent was left to stare at a blank stage.

After an uncomfortably long five minutes, the great John of God walked on stage.

As the silent crowd got on their feet to cheer, I did my best not to drop my jaw. The noise coming from the crowd contained sounds I had never heard before. The silent mass of humans transformed into congregants in a revival tent, speaking in tongues. It was a little terrifying. Some people raised their hands and wailed guttural animal sounds, while others fell to their knees and cried. Some made keening sounds as they rocked back and forth, looking up as if God himself had entered the tent. All of the sounds of salvation. I turned to my mother to see that she, too, had gotten caught up in the moment.

The John of God from the videos, that amiable guy who could work a room and perform psychic surgeries with a smile, had changed dramatically. Who I saw was different. The John of God in front of us was a large man who lumbered out dressed all in white. He was bloated to the point that his white shoes were not able to lace properly. In previous pictures, he wore short-sleeved button-down shirts that showed healthy arms and a trim figure. This John of God had unkempt hair dyed jet black and was not able to walk unaided. He wore a three-quarter-length white denim coat, a white scarf, white pants and shoes. I knew my mom was the sickest person in the audience, but I had to admit that John of God almost looked in worse shape. He looked nothing like the guy in the videos. That guy, who channeled Entities whenever he wanted, walked around his Casa and said hi to everyone, laughed, and seemed rather charming.

The attendants claimed John of God could not walk unassisted when he was channeling the Entities. It seemed like a cover. This was an extremely unhealthy man who was not capable of standing on his own. It was a little odd watching the attendants struggle to keep him upright. Being told one thing when I knew we had seen the opposite was disconcerting at best. It was apparent that the Entities had more than an audience to cure—they had to work on their number one channeler. His extremities were swollen and his ankles were puffy. He looked like bloated Elvis before he died.

I looked at Laurie first, and she looked right back at me with the same expression. Disbelief, like we were watching a scene from "The Emperor's New Clothes." Everyone around us was ecstatic just to have him standing there. I was not convinced. I kept wrinkling my nose, thinking I smelled a rat. Were they seriously going to continue a three-day seminar with a man who could barely keep his eyes open? The attendants on either side of him paraded John of God around the stage as he muttered incoherently. Someone translated, saying he was blessing everyone. I looked to my left, and my mom had the same expression as the rest of those in the audience. She looked at me with the eyes of a child. Her tiny face behind those big glasses looked like a little Catholic girl who had seen Jesus himself.

In a voice as tiny as my daughter's, she exclaimed in a whisper, "He's here! Look, that's him! I can't believe we're here, can you? Oh my God, this is amazing! Look at him!" She was overjoyed. She was absolutely mesmerized.

Within a blink, he was gone.

Was that it? All this for a gravely ill old man shuffling around the stage, mumbling incoherent blessings?

I was on my tippy-toes trying to see what was going on. He had disappeared with the two attendants. The braided woman came out again. After all the positive and electrifying energy of the participants had subsided, she made an important announcement. The individual blessings would begin. If anyone had sent pictures to Brazil, had surgery scheduled, chemo to begin, or anything else medical coming up that required an immediate blessing, they should move to the right side of the tent.

OK, I thought, now we're getting somewhere. It was clear that whoever was the worst off would get in first. Judging from the crowd lining up, there were either a lot of fakers or there were more sick people than I had realized. I collected my mom and the wheelchair and we made our way to the right side of the tent where there was a makeshift hallway. My mom was in a bubble of joy. I was determined not to let my increasingly bad attitude impact her time there, even as I kept casting knowing looks at Laurie. She just shook her head. It wasn't what she had imagined either. She whispered to me that she thought John of God had advanced heart disease given his edema. I thought maybe he had the flu.

This tented hallway led outside into the bright, warm, breezy daylight. In front of us was a long building. I looked around for a wheelchair entrance, but there was none. When I asked about it, I was instructed to leave the wheelchair outside, along with all our bags. I didn't think anything would get stolen, but I had no idea how long we would be in there. I was a little nervous to be without all my mom's medications. How could there not be a handicapped entrance and special attention to the severely ill on the compound of the visiting faith healer? Wasn't everyone there for a miracle? Why wasn't this made easier?

Laurie and I held my mother's elbows and guided her up the stairs into the building. It was a large, rectangular space divided into four equal parts by sheer screens. Again, we were instructed to be silent, since now we were in what was called the current room. It was supposed to be supercharged with spiritual energy that would heal us.

We passed through the first division, where some pilgrims had been seated, silently praying or meditating. The second division was empty. More attendants were there to line us up properly so we could approach the third division. Of equal size, this one was a little different. There were rows of chairs like in the previous two divisions, but this one held a small area resembling an altar. It was a decent-sized platform draped in lots of yellow fabric and held a throne where John of God was supposed to sit. We were not really supposed to have our eyes open; nor were we to look directly at the altar. Of course I did. I didn't understand why all of this was shrouded in such mystery. My mom was diligent, though, so I held her arm as she walked, eyes closed, towards the altar. On it were statues of people I didn't recognize but assumed represented the Entities. We were instructed only to pass by it, not stop in front of it. We were then guided to seats in the third and fourth divisions. There was no rhyme or reason to the seating. It looked like we were supposed to sit in the third section and await whatever blessing was to be bestowed upon us, and then move to the fourth one before we were funneled outside.

As we approached the altar, John of God was not present. My guess is he had to rest before he walked around and blessed everyone. Just passing by where he was to sit was purported to be enough by John of God's attendants, because we were told to sit in this section. I kept my head down so I wouldn't be busted for being defiant, but I definitely had my eyes open. I wanted to see what he did! I saw a bunch of feet shuffling him around, some mumbling in some language I didn't recognize, and then someone telling us we were finished. It occurred to me that we had been asked to keep our eyes closed because the Great Healer was so gravely ill, we might have been frightened by his condition. I felt like we were all part of a great charade and had to pretend we were feeling better by just being in his presence. Maybe doing all that research and video watching wasn't such a great idea. Maybe if I had gone into the week with no previous knowledge, I would have been more open. But I had. And I wanted to see the kind-faced healer from the videos, the one who seemed to connect with his pilgrims.

All I ended up thinking was, Really? That's it? No touching of the head or shoulder with words that we could remember, like "Peace be with you" or "Feel better" or "You're cured"?

Nothing?

I could not believe that we had been there for less than an hour and we were done. I asked Laurie if she felt anything; she said she felt a lot of positive energy and that she was safe. I felt the total opposite. I felt angry and cheated.

Another woman spoke in a clear, soothing voice: "You have received your first spiritual intervention. Now you will go outside for a decompression session. Only there will you be able to ask questions."

Outside stood the same overall-wearing attendant who had shushed us inside the tent. Certainly that was a sign of something unfortunate yet to come. I sized him up a bit better as we found our seats. He was a cross between a Disneyland employee who had seen too many crying children and a Catholic school nun waiting to crack knuckles with a ruler. He was smug, a bit of a know-it-all, and had the impatience of someone who had already answered too many questions. He did not look like he was remotely interested in any of the questions that were about to be fired at him. It was clear he wanted to complete his task and move on to something more interesting. I had no idea if this guy had been in Brazil with John of God and had come with that entourage or if he was a local paid to dress in white and tell us what to do. I did know that there was not one empathetic bone in his little body based on how he stood before us with his arms folded over his chest, hips to the side and head slightly up. It was his lack of eye contact that made me really think this guy was not part of the healer's inner circle. If he had been, I hoped he would have been a little more approachable.

His rehearsed speech, filled with a lot of heavy sighs, told us that now that we had received our blessing and intervention, our psyches and souls were wide open and we should not talk to or absorb anyone else's energy for the next twenty-four hours. We were instructed to go back to our hotels, sleep as much as possible, and only receive food that no one else had touched. If it were possible to abstain from food and water altogether, it would be better for the blessing. We should remain in our white clothing. We should not watch TV. We should not bathe.

After he was done with this list of rules, he was open to questions. There were some fascinating ones like, "I am staying at a hotel. If I get hungry, how can I get food that no one else touches?" It was a logical question, but it frustrated the smug attendant, who expelled another heavy sigh. "Just tell room service to leave it outside the door. Next question." There were less intelligent ones that showed the person just hadn't listened. "Can I drink water that no one touches?" "Yes, just turn on the tap."

I went up to the guy after and asked him if there were any breakout sessions or activities in the afternoon. Since we had come all the way from California, and my mom was dying, we wanted a little more experience while we were there. I thought maybe there was yoga or meditation or massages. He told me that my mother could rest in one of the cottages set up for people to relax and nap, but that was about it. There was no massage, no crystal healing, and no music. I then asked if it were possible to get a private audience with John of God. We of course would make a donation to the Brazil operation if we could get a moment of his time. I did my best agenting, but this guy was not buying any of it. He told me that I could not expect to see John with all the other people wanting the same thing, and besides, when he's not channeling the Entities, he was just like any other businessman.

Cue record scratching across the turntable.

"Seriously," I replied. "Really. Like a businessman? Wow, that's not what I expected to hear."

He replied, clenching his jaw, "Well, you really should just pay attention and get with our program."

Without missing a beat, I shot back, "Honey, after what I've seen today, I think my program trumps yours any day." I turned on my heels and did my best to peel out of there in hopes of spraying his whites with some sod and mud.

Making sure my angry energy did not disrupt her open aura, I calmly explained to my mother that she was advised to go home. No entering the main tent to pray with the people who had not been blessed, since they were still throwing off their bad energy. I suggested she could take a nap back at the hotel and then we could walk around town. She was up for that but said, "I saw a shop by the entrance—let's go there first, since Joanne and the kids would want something."

Well, so much for keeping the soul clean. Retail energy would certainly mess up her healing, but Nancy never passed up a good shopping opportunity. She bought blessed water for Joanne, even though it was only city water bottled in Poughkeepsie. She bought bracelets with specific healing stones for the kids, a few books, and some other branded crap that was totally unnecessary.

After a good half hour in the store, I attempted to usher my mom out so her open chakras wouldn't become clouded by the inflated prices. I am sure John of God made a killing on all the merchandising. She wrapped up her purchases and I went to get the car. It took about ten minutes to get back to the hotel, and it was the drive alone that calmed me down. The three of us were in our own mental spaces as we made the right onto the street that would take us back to the hotel. For me, I played the game with myself that I had played on any road trip I had ever taken: look for the things outside that held the greatest beauty. It was a fail-safe game that always made me feel better. The first thing I saw was the falling red and yellow leaves. What could be more beautiful than that? Maybe the thick trees and carpets of green grass, but that was all trumped by a turtle crossing the road. I'd never seen that before. If I had been alone, I would have gotten out of the car and put it on the side of the road. But I wasn't. So I settled on the turtle being the most beautiful thing I'd seen that day. The brisk air was the capper on my stress. Everything fell away as I thought about nothing other than the chilled air and the beautiful surroundings. I wondered for a split second why I was so preoccupied with finding spirituality amongst strangers.

CHAPTER EIGHT

We decided to meet at the lobby of the hotel for breakfast. The trek to the cafeteria at the Omega Center was more than we wanted to do again, and I was still feeling slightly put off about the previous day.

My mom was already sitting at a table in the middle of the crowded dining room, with a little bit of yogurt and some tea, trying to look like she was perfectly healthy and enjoying herself. But she was wearing a painful smile that was becoming more transparent as the cancer progressed, and it seemed to be moving quickly, even over the course of a couple days on our trip. It was evident the joy from the previous day had worn off. Something must have happened before I got there, because the energy surrounding her was a bit off. Laurie was a little bit frantic, trying to get some food into my mom. I was so relieved there was someone else there to help out. One of my fears on this trip was being alone with my mom and having something go wrong. My stress was alleviated by Laurie's ability to do just about anything. Not only was she the trained professional with cancer patients, Laurie was now the person I could talk to about my mom and about our experience.

I was about to follow Laurie to the breakfast buffet to find out how the morning had gone and to see what she had to say about the previous night's sleep, but as I began to stand up, my mom started coughing.

It wasn't just a little cough; it was a phlegm-filled rattle that was so disturbing that the people at the next table looked over, horrified. It started out like a clear-your-throat kind of cough. She did that a few times. But then her face turned red. She was trying to stifle a larger, more disturbing cough. I know she was embarrassed that she was becoming the center of unwanted attention, but she was also terrified she was going to choke to death. I knew the latter was not going to happen, since she was breathing in between coughs. She had worked herself up into a panic, which was something I had never seen before. As my mom's panic escalated, I became calmer. She wasn't sure if she should push away from the table and run or sit there and tough it out. I put my hand on top of hers as she gripped the edge of the table. I calmly assured her that she would not suffocate, that she would be all right. Laurie came rushing over and asked me what had happened. I wanted to break my calm exterior and cry, scoop up my mom and take her to the hospital, but it was clear that sort of drama was not warranted. As calmly as Laurie asked me what had happened, I responded in an equal tone, hoping my mom would absorb the lack of panic in front of her. Laurie rubbed my mom's back and told her she would be all right, just to focus for a second to try to slow the coughing. She listened and tried, but I could tell she was terrified.

It was one of those moments where I was suddenly aware of every aspect of the room. My senses had heightened as I took in the waitress in the corner with her pad and pen, poised to make sure she didn't have to call 911; the smell of burning toast at the breakfast buffet from the lady in the polyester slacks and warm-hued sweater. The receding hairline and silver-rimmed glasses of the man at the next table not certain what he should do; the spoon that had fallen out of the yogurt cup, spreading boysenberry yogurt on the maroon tablecloth; the feel of the paper napkin in the hand not holding my mom's. All eyes were on us as my mom sounded like she was cracking ribs with the force of her cough. She had choked on her pills as she was trying to swallow them, nothing more than that.

Silver-Rimmed Glasses looked relieved once the coughing stopped and asked if there was anything he could do. He was standing up as his sentence came out, like he was going to spring into action on our behalf. He offered to get a glass of water or to call a doctor. I assured him that we didn't need either and thanked him for his kindness. Once the coughing stopped, I believe it was the quickest my mother had moved in weeks. The fear of suffocating, and the sheer embarrassment of such a sight in a public restaurant, was enough to catapult her out the door. Laurie managed to gather everything up and got us ready to go. Her instincts were right on as my mom collected herself, stood up like nothing had happened, and walked quickly to the car.

Fresh air. Somehow it made everything that much less difficult. I followed my mom, who had gotten a ridiculous burst of energy, like she had cheated death. She was moving so fast. She waited at the car, wearing a smile that was both triumphant and afraid. I understood exactly how she felt, because I, too, felt like we had just escaped the Grim Reaper. Looking her over and gently acknowledging that that experience was frightening, I got in the car and we sped off to the Omega Center.

We had a good idea the day's activities would be similar to those of the day before. I was starting to wonder why we were bothering to go again. But my mom wanted to get as much spiritual intervention as possible. We parked in the same area, unloaded the wheelchair and all the bags, got my mom comfortable, and headed to the cart to take us up the hill. We bypassed the same unfortunate woman at the check-in desk, hoping to start the morning on a more positive and healing note. The morning unfolded the same as it had the day before. It was oddly silent again in the tent as everyone waited. I felt less engaged this time, not having any expectation that this experience would grant me the spiritual connectedness I longed for. My mom, though, was as engaged as ever, watching the stage like she was waiting for her favorite rock star. When the braided lady came out, she did not have John of God with her. She instructed us again to line up if we needed immediate blessings. It was clear the routine would be the same, and I was grateful we sat closer to the makeshift hallway so we could get our blessing and move on with the day.

We went through the current rooms, but this time John of God was sitting on his throne. Although we were instructed not to open our eyes, I of course did. There he was, slouching to the side in that low, wide chair, looking even less healthy than before. He looked completely disinterested to the point where I thought he might be napping. His head was down, his hands casually lying on the armrests. His legs were parted and his shoes looked like they had been wedged onto his swollen feet. He had on the same outfit, which was odd, since it was rather warm in the room. I was sure his heavy scarf had to be uncomfortable. Once we shuffled past him, we sat down with our eyes closed. A woman came through and informed us we had completed our spiritual interventions. My mouth twitched back and forth like I was going to burst into some inappropriate accusation about how my time was being wasted, but I stopped myself. I was there for my mom, who seemed completely satisfied with her experience.

Afterwards, we were funneled out of the John of God area like dazed cattle. I was prepared to leave the Omega Center and head back to the hotel, since the day before my mom had had little interest in hanging out. I thought it would be nice if she and I walked around town, but she had other plans. My mom wanted to hang out for a bit, take a nap, and maybe have lunch there. I understood her motivations, even though I would have preferred to have some actual time with her outside the Omega Center. This trip had been so important to her, it would have been a shame for me to impose my needs and pull her away from time at the center.

I asked someone where we could relax and was instructed to take my mom up to the tree-flanked cabin at the top of the hill, designated for resting. It was a beautiful fall day. Thankfully, getting up to the cabin was easy. There was a paved path that went right to the door. The grass was green. The air was crisp enough for a light sweater, but the sun was warm enough that if we decided to stay outside, we would be comfortable. We made our way up the hill, remarking on how lovely it was to be on the East Coast that time of year. We lamented the lack of leaf-changing in Los Angeles, the smog, the heat, and anything else we could think of to make it feel like being in Rhinebeck, New York, was the greatest choice we had ever made. As we got closer to the cabin, we could see through the huge windows next to the front door that it was dark inside.

My mom was a little skeptical, but Laurie and I said we would check it out.

There was no one in charge of the cabin. There were only rows of low cots with military blankets folded neatly on each, though it was warm enough in there that they weren't needed. Between the cots were thick yoga mats being used by pilgrims. To the right of the door, against the inside wall below two large windows, were stacks of extra mats and blankets in case someone wanted to double up. Almost every cot was taken, except for one directly opposite the stacks of mats and blankets. My mom chose that one as Laurie and I sat on the floor beside her. We took note of the time my mom lay down, conscious of her fluctuating blood sugar. She soon settled in for what would be a very long nap.

At first I thought I would take advantage of the quiet time to try my best meditation skills. But there was just too much commotion with people settling in. They were trying to be quiet so as not to disturb the other resting pilgrims. However, the person making the most noise was my restless mother. She was actually waking people up with whatever she was dreaming. People were sitting up on their cots, trying to figure out who was making all the noise, a few even trying to shush her. I watched everyone watching her, some of them frustrated enough that they got up and left, muttering under their breath. She was moving more than I had seen her move as of late. Usually she just made hand gestures that accompanied unintelligible sounds that had the cadence of a conversation. But this time, she was really active. It sounded like she was having a spirited conversation with someone and she was determined to convince them of something. Her feet were moving as well. It was a little disturbing watching this but, at the same time, fascinating.

In my fantasy, she was talking to her deceased brother, her parents, her fabulous and naughty friend Kathy, who always made her laugh, and her friend Donald, who had died from pancreatic cancer years before. I imagined that these spirit guides were telling her that the other side was much more fun than living with cancer, that she should come join them soon, and that they would be there to help her make the transition. Thinking this actually brought me a lot of comfort. It was helpful to imagine that when it was her time to go, she would have friends and family welcoming her. She wouldn't be afraid to leave. Instead, she would be welcomed to eternity by those who loved her. She would be able to meet famous souls from the past and could travel anywhere she wanted, whenever she wanted.

Whatever the medical explanation was for this moment, I was going with mine because it was far more romantic and interesting and certainly a conversation starter. If you could pick your spirit guides to help you transition out of life, who would they be? I'd have my mom, my grandmother, and Cleopatra.

I looked over at Laurie, who had been watching my mom's movements, curious as to what her explanation would be.

I whispered, "Do you know why she does this?"

Laurie said such movement was common at the end of people's lives when they were on large amounts of morphine. I was disappointed with this answer. Laurie and I had both witnessed my mom thinking she saw a ghost. I didn't want to debate it, so I let it go. Instead, I asked her to come outside with me. We both got up and sat on the bench outside the big picture window next to the front door so we could keep an eye on my mom.

Soaking up the late-morning sun, I asked Laurie what had happened before I came in to breakfast. She told me my mom had had a difficult night's sleep and had been frustrated when she finally woke. It was the second night my mom had spent hours in front of her computer screen, touching it like she was seeing something that Laurie could not. She watched my mom try to put her hand into the screen, the blue light reflecting into the room with an eerie glow. My mom was not aware that Laurie was there. She was in her own world, looking intently into the screen. Both nights had gone the same. Laurie took my mom's temperature and blood pressure and listened to her cloudy lungs. She tested her blood sugar and said goodnight to my mom as she was climbing into bed. She listened to my mom snore lightly as she fell asleep to the evening news.

While Laurie was preparing herself for bed, my mom got up and turned off the TV and sat at the desk where her computer was. Wanting to keep a watchful eye, Laurie kept the connecting door open a tiny bit. Both nights had been the same. Laurie was expecting my mom to close her computer and go back to bed, like she had the night before, but last night, my mom sat hunched in the chair with her face close to the computer screen. Laurie said she saw wispy objects floating around my mom. She said she had never seen anything like it before. Instead of being afraid, Laurie was certain that my mom was being watched over.

I got a wonderful chill that confirmed I had been right. I knew my mom was having conversations in her sleep. I told Laurie about Melida seeing ghosts on the security camera screen in the kitchen at my mom's house.

Laurie calmly stated that we have no idea what happens when someone is dying. It was the first time she had used that word to describe my mom's condition. It was comforting and sad at the same time. I wanted an explanation that made sense, but more importantly, I wanted validation that what I was thinking wasn't insane. I hadn't been able to talk to anyone about my mom like that before.

For all the conversations I had had with my brothers about the end of my mom's life, even with all the fevers, frailty, and medications, it had never really occurred to me until the moment I spoke to Laurie that my invincible mother would actually die. I imagined she would die like an actress in a movie, then come back to do another role. But her actually ceasing to exist was not part of my equation. She could "die" like when my brothers and I played Cowboys and Indians, but not die and cease to be a physical part of our lives. I really thought she could pull through, fall in love with someone fantastic, and live long enough to see my kids go to college. She hadn't inherited her father's family's bad genetics of heart disease and Alzheimer's or the depression of her mother's side. She was supposed to live a long life. Pancreatic cancer was nowhere in her family, so she had to be the anomaly that lived an excellent life after diagnosis. Maybe this would be her low point before things started to pick up. I could picture her in her eighties, zipping around in her little Mercedes, changing the world for unfortunate children. Julianna would be next to her, all grown up, listening as my mom set the example of how my daughter should conduct her life.

I had terrible, conflicting feelings I couldn't yet express. I was devastated that my deep sense of denial was crumbling around me. I was relieved that my mom's suffering would end soon and felt horribly guilty for it at the same time. My mother was going to die. No one knew when, but I was certain her death was coming sooner than I wanted it to.

It was a lot for me to take in, so I took my journal with me and told Laurie I was going to explore the grounds. I would meet her back in a half hour. I was doing my best to remain calm in front of Laurie. Last thing I wanted her to think was that she had to take care of me as well. So I walked quickly away, afraid if I went slowly, Laurie would hear my sobs. I wasn't prepared to be that vulnerable with her. I needed to be alone.

The sobs came quickly and uncontrollably. I was going to lose my mom and I didn't know what to do with the sadness that overcame me. I walked quickly head down, clutching my pencil and my black journal, looking for a private spot to shield me from others. Stifling sobs never turned out well for me. I ended up making snorting sounds that drew more attention than I wanted. They were sounds from deep within, ones that felt so good to release once I let it all go. I looked up the hill at a bunch of trees, hoping there would be enough privacy there for me to sit and cry as much as I wanted. I could cry for the pain experienced by my mom, my children, and myself. I could cry for Mike never seeing my mom without cancer. I could cry that for the rest of my life, I wouldn't have her to call when something good happened. I cried for the future holidays, the milestones of my children's lives that would not be shared with her. I cried for not knowing who I was supposed to be without her.

The more I climbed up the hill, hoping to find a spot to fall to my knees so I could dig my hands into the leaves, the better I felt. I walked as far as I could. The more I let everything out, the more I felt I was going to be all right with whatever lay ahead. I must have walked around for twenty-five minutes, wandering among the small private cabins and eventually making it up to the yoga pavilion. There was a sunny spot with a bench, so I sat there looking at the fountain in front of me. I noticed there were frogs in it, so I took pictures to show my kids.

They liked that sort of thing. It made me feel better too.

The frustration I felt in the tent that morning, those controlling people from the day before, the lack of mojo I was feeling from the experience, slipped away as I listened to the water and watched the frogs. Maybe this place was the sign. Maybe needing to be outside to find my center was enough. Maybe I didn't need any more than that. Couldn't that be enough?

I sat for a few minutes thinking about that when I realized my time was up. I walked back down to the resting cabin to find that my mom was still asleep. I told Laurie I was going to wander some more and come back in another half hour, so she could get up and stretch her legs. I wandered into the bookstore, looking for a new journal that would forever remind me of my experience, but couldn't find one. I walked over past the statue in our photo, into the garden where birds were pecking at the last of the seeds left from the summer vegetables. I sat on a weathered Adirondack chair, watching them for a bit, thinking about my moment of clarity. The sun felt so nice on my face and I was starting to feel more relaxed. There were no people around; they were all still waiting for their blessings, or resting beyond the tent on the expansive green lawn. Just me, the rustle of falling leaves, the sunshine, and the chatter of birds. My shoulders relaxed, my restlessness was waning, and I finally slipped into a meditative state that I realized had previously only been achieved when I was in the garden.

The simple act of watching Nature in action, the birds preparing for winter, the bees doing the same, and the falling leaves protecting the garden soil from a disruptive freeze was really what it took for me to calm down. It was so simple.

I gave up, for the moment, being so hard on myself. Why bother with beating myself up for not being spiritual enough when I had a dying mom and an uncertain emotional future? Why not revel in the things that made me smile? I hoped I was done with feeling guilty about not being a better Jew. I would be home soon enough to continue Gemilut Hasadim with my fellow congregants. Why not just take what impacted me most about being a Jew and remain mindful of my actions? I decided if I was going to be a better Jew, what I really needed was to practice the same acts of loving kindness on myself.

Content with my new thoughts of what might be my sense of connectedness to something greater, I got up from my sunny spot and moved back towards my dying mother.

| CHAPTER NINE |

My mom finally woke three hours later, feeling rested and ready to move on to something different. I suggested she and I go for a little walk in town for lunch. Laurie deserved a break, since she'd been with my mom for forty-eight hours straight. My mom would have to take it slow, since Laurie had noticed her oxygen levels were very low.

When we got back to the hotel, I slowly walked my mom around to the main street and meandered into a restaurant just finishing its lunch rush. My mom of course ordered an ice cream sundae and I ordered a soup. We had been having light conversation about what was happening at home. I didn't have anything exciting to report, just the routines of my children.

I took this opportunity to ask her if she remembered her dreams. She smiled and told me she did not, but was curious why. I told her how I had watched her dreaming earlier that day and thought she was having intense conversations with someone; she was intrigued and would try to remember next time. I took it a step further, testing the waters to see how far I could go with this uncharted line of discussion. I had not talked to her before about anything closely resembling death when she was sick. We had talked about it before she had cancer, in a matter-of-fact sort of way, in case she died while traveling or was killed in an accident. I knew her burial plans and the details of her estate. But we had not talked about anything emotional surrounding her death. It was the no-fly zone of our relationship.

In as gentle and caring a way as possible, I told her I hoped she was talking to her dad, the kindest man she knew. I shared my hope that the ghosts from her past were paying a visit to help her get ready for the next chapter. She actually liked that idea and we talked a little bit more about whom she would see. We reminisced about family members long gone and laughed about old times when we lived in New Jersey. I was so happy to have that time with her. Perhaps, I thought, I could take it even further and talk to her about how much I loved her. I thought I could tell her how important the trip had been for our relationship. Instead, since I was not quite ready for that, I told her to say hi to a bunch of people I missed. We laughed a comfortable laugh, then let the conversation flow to other less important topics, like what turned out to be the meager shopping in town.

It didn't take much to tire her out, so, arm in arm, we shuffled back to the room so I could help her pack. We had made a plan to get everything in the car and check out of the hotel before I dropped her and Laurie at the Omega Center in the morning. My friend Tracie was coming down from Vermont for lunch, so I would not be staying past the spiritual intervention.

I planned on picking them up around lunchtime, then calling the plane to see if we could leave early and hitting the road back home.

While we were packing, unsolicited, my mom started talking about our relationship. She looked rather wistful as she began to talk, as I folded her things and put them in her suitcase. She told me how important it was that I was there with her for this trip. There were no tears, just gratitude for being there with her. Few words, and they were meaningful. I knew this trip was hard on her emotionally and physically. Her cough had gotten worse and she felt weak from her low oxygen levels. I couldn't imagine she wanted to go home to face what little of her life remained, as hospice lay on the horizon. This was our last hurrah. So she ended by telling me that even with life, cancer, and death swirling around us, the most important thing in her life was our relationship.

I was touched by how transparent my mom had become, because it was not easy for her to be so straightforward with her feelings. The irony was that she had always made a point to tell my brothers and me to always openly discuss our feelings. Good or bad, my mom always knew how the three of us felt. This was one of the reasons why not being able to talk to her about how I felt during her illness was so difficult.

Maybe a month prior to our trip, I had asked my mom if I could go with her to her therapist. I'd done this in the past; we were a family where therapy was no stranger. We went to each other's shrinks, sat in on each other's group therapy, and if we weren't taking verbal beatings for how awful we had behaved, we were being apologized to from the person sharing for being such a shit.

I had been so bent out of shape about how my mom constantly shut me out of her life when I showed any emotion.

Since we were getting ready for this trip, I thought it would be smart to do the difficult work of discussing with my mom and her therapist how I felt. I wanted to talk to my mom about her dying. I was so resentful of how she had treated her own health. She paid no attention to her diet; she ate more sugar as a victim of pancreatic cancer than she had when she was healthy. As far as I was concerned, she had a death wish. While I wrestled with not wanting to pass judgment on how she lived her cancer life, I was positive that if I had been in her shoes, I would have changed my behaviors to make sure I would live as long as possible. Once her pancreas was removed and she no longer manufactured insulin, the idea that she would have to forgo dessert was clearly more than she could take. So she ate whatever sugar she wanted and calculated her insulin around that. I was furious with the doctor who suggested this was an acceptable way to live with cancer and diabetes. I was also mad at her for not being able to use the word "cancer." I didn't know if she was protecting us from how bad it really was or if she was burying her head in a bowl of Häagen-Dazs Dulce de Leche because she refused to see the truth. I was her grown-up daughter, who happened to be a very angry child. I was restricted from continuing my relationship with her as it had always been. Cancer had gotten in the way of it, instead of bringing us closer together. I missed my mom and she wasn't even dead yet.

I had heard of so many people not being able to settle things with their parents before they died, so they remained in limbo, stuck forever. I didn't want that to happen to me. I wanted the end of my mom's life to be complete with me, like it had been with my grandmother. I missed her all the time, but we had completed our relationship in the best way possible. I had no more unanswered questions. So I needed my mom to hear me.

It was a calculated risk entering that office. I weighed my options, since I could end up completely cut off. I decided our relationship was worth a fight, no matter how hard it was to speak the words. And, I had to be OK with whatever tears were shed. I planned to pour my heart out. I wanted to sound empathetic and sad, yet angry at the same time.

So when the shrink asked me how I felt about my mom's cancer, I told her.

"As her child, I cry every day. I walk around with an enormous amount of sadness that she's going to die. I am in my car listening to songs on the radio and I cry because it reminds me of times when we were together. I have become comfortable with the amount I cry. I mostly do it alone, but I do it every day without fail. It's the only way I can get through the day. When I am not sad, I am angry. Angry that she is so sick that she can't be with her grandchildren anymore. I am furious that when I have emotions about her cancer in front of her, I get cut out of what time she has left. I have to balance all those emotions with my marriage, my children, and my job."

I grabbed a handful of tissues, crying through the words.

"I have become so good at talking through my tears that I am not even embarrassed when I cry. All I say is, 'My mom has cancer.' Everyone understands why I cry. But my mom doesn't. She won't let me. It's the worst feeling I've ever had, not being able to talk to her about how much I miss who she used to be, or how I am going to miss her. Or how I wish I could know everything about what's going on so I can figure out how to be prepared for when she is not here anymore."

My mom was visibly shaken by what I said. She began on the defense and interjected that she felt I was devoid of emotion when I talked about her situation. I went on to say that I knew from experience that if I didn't pretend I was OK, she would stop sharing. I had to remain the strong one and then go complain to my brothers or cry with my husband.

I told the therapist that as her daughter, the person she had raised me to be, I wanted my mom to fight a little harder. She taught us to fight with everything we had for the things we believed in. It's how she lived her life, up until cancer. I wanted her to live a more healthy life so she could hang on to see the kids grow up a bit more. I asked her if she just didn't care about living anymore, since her actions seemed so self-destructive.

I was on a roll and couldn't stop. All the anger I had was coming out. I thought we would have more than one discussion over the course of a few sessions, but I vomited everything up in that moment. It felt great.

Once it was clear I had finished, the therapist said, "Now's the time. Get it all out now, because you don't have that much time left. If you have something to say, just say it."

So in the hotel room in Rhinebeck, New York, my mother took the therapist's advice. She told me that I'd been the best daughter she ever could have asked for. She listed the things she loved and admired most: my individuality, my ability to love, my discerning eye, and my ability to say what needed saying. I smiled as she listed my qualities, like I had never heard them before. I was still, for once, relishing the love she was expressing. I vowed to be clear with her. If time was indeed running out, then I wanted to make sure I had everything answered.

So, while folding the endless amounts of clothing to be placed in the suitcase, I started to cry, still feeling like I had been a disappointment.

"I am sorry I wasn't more like you. I am sorry I was mean to you when I was a teenager and really sorry for being so angry when you and dad got divorced. You have been the best role model for me with Julianna. I don't want you to die;

I want you to get better. I want you to see the kids grow up and I want you to get to know Mike. He's an incredible man who loves me no matter what. He loves me the way you do. Whatever happens, I want to be with you. Please make sure I am with you when you die. I don't think I could handle not being with you when you die. Please. I will be there with you no matter what, I promise. I can take care of you. It's what I want to do. Please."

I felt like a disaster of a child and regretted every negative thing I had ever thought about my mom. Who was I to be so judgmental on how she lived her life? Christ, I should just be grateful I even had such fabulous parents. I always accepted them for who they were, never demanding anything from them. Maybe it was a holdover from being adopted. I was always afraid to rock the boat too much in case they decided to give me back. Some wounds never heal.

As I was crying, she moved closer to me on the edge of the bed. She touched my hands and said with the most serene face I'd seen in a year that she loved me. She said I was perfect. I never disappointed her. I had always been so good, even when I wasn't. I smiled and cried some more. She told me she might not be able to control the circumstances of her death, but if she could, she would wait for me to be there. Then I reached across the bed and gave my little bony mother a hug. I told her I loved her too.

We continued packing in silence for a few minutes. Then I asked her what she had hoped to get out of her time with John of God.

She looked at me with total clarity and said, "I want to be cured."

I pondered this for a few minutes. Cured of what? Surely she knew she was dying. Cured of her inner demons? Absolved of something greater that only God could know? I asked, "Cured of what?"

"Cancer," she said, a little annoyed.

How could I not see that coming? She had been in denial for so long, why would now be any different? I remained speechless for more time than I should have. I had no idea what to say. I was astounded by how out of touch she was with her current stage of life. At the same time, I was also inspired by her faith that John of God was going to be the answer for her. I was afraid I was going to say something sarcastic, since my experience had clearly not lived up to hers.

Instead, I smiled. "I hope you're right. That would be great," I said, turning away from her to put the remaining clothes into her suitcase. I was afraid my face would betray me.

Her statement confirmed that I had to do more for my mom with this trip. I wanted to arrange for her to see John of God on her own, regardless of who he was offstage. If her wish was going to come true, I was going to do my best to make sure I did everything in my power to help it along. I wanted the both of us to live happily ever after. Now was the time to get all I could out of this John of God experience.

I wanted my mom to have her miracle.

∽

When Laurie came back, she stayed with my mom while I called Carole, who, strangely enough, seemed completely prepared for my call. She was happy to hear from me, told me she did not want to insert herself into my time with my mom, but was thrilled with the update on the trip and the opportunity to help do something more. I told Carole how the trip had gone thus far, leaving out any of my negativity. In my description of how it wasn't quite what I had expected, I told Carole that I wanted my mom to have a moment with him alone.

There is no one else like Carole. She can get anything accomplished. She asks a million questions to make sure she has all the knowledge available. If I am ever sick in the hospital, I am putting Carole in charge of my medical care. She knows how to get the best out of everyone and does it with pure style and charm.

Within minutes, Carole had me on conference call with a local woman, Patricia, who occasionally put John of God up at her house. I don't know how she did it, but it felt like she had all the pieces in place in case I had called. Patricia explained the procedure for things at the Omega Center, which was pretty much what I had already done. Carole interjected that she and I wanted more for my mom. We both got a little dramatic and said it was my mom's dying wish to see him. As I explained my mom's failing health, Carole interjected, "Can she have a psychic surgery?"

This was not what I had been looking for at all. I had no interest in subjecting my mom to something so unpredictable and unsafe. The psychic surgery participants I had seen in videos all looked way more healthy. I envisioned my mom in some trance while John of God inserted some scary thing up her nose to pull out the demons or something equally as frightening. I interrupted Carole, and in the strongest voice I could muster, squashed that notion altogether. I didn't even allow Patricia to answer the question. The thought of it made me shudder. However, I had to hand it to Carole. She was willing to do anything for my mom, including asking for something that was considered illegal in our country.

Eventually, Patricia was willing to give us a private audience with John of God so my mom could ask him one question. It was the only thing she said she could do. I had a feeling from the tone in her voice that she just wanted to get us off the phone. I was told to look for a woman named Kathy after we received our initial blessing in the morning. I was to tell her about my conversation with Patricia, who gave my mom the OK to ask John of God one question. I was about to negotiate for more questions but decided not to push it. I knew my mom would have a hard time coming up with just one question she didn't already know the answer to. I thanked Patricia profusely. She hung up, and Carole and I discussed how I would help my mother prepare. I was elated that I could do something more meaningful for my mom.

i

I awoke with energy on the great Day of the Question. Two things had me smiling before I was fully awake: The first was that the next night, I would be home in my own bed with my family snuggling and watching TV. Second was the cliff-hanger of the day—what would she ask John of God? After the lack of conversation around it the night before, I thought maybe she simply had no idea herself. All she said was, she was just happy to have been appointed a special task and said she would think of something as she approached. When we met at the car, everyone was in excellent spirits, even though my mom's cough seemed to be getting worse.

We cruised into the muddy parking lot right on time. I dropped Laurie, my mom, and the wheelchair at the entrance, parked the car, and we began our walk to the big white tent. After the first blessings, I quickly approached a female attendant and asked for Kathy. When I was introduced to her, I told her I had spoken to Patricia and relayed the entire conversation regarding the question. While I was excited my mom was about to get the special treatment I had set up for her, Patricia distractedly nodded and directed us to get in line where everyone else was. Again, I was put off by her indifference. But for the sake of my mom, I shoved any ill feelings down as far as I could.

We were lined up to go into the current rooms when Kathy announced to everyone else around us that we could all ask one question of John of God. There was not going to be any special treatment for my mom, like I was led to believe. I had been yessed to my heart's content the day before by someone who just wanted to get me off the phone. My disappointment was turning into some real anger, since I had been led to believe that something special was going to happen exclusively for my mom. Laurie shot me a questioning look, knowing something had happened. All I could muster were the words, "I got totally screwed by these people."

My grip on the wheelchair handles was turning my knuckles white. I was furious. I wanted to enter the current rooms filled with anger to see what would happen. Would my fury ripple through all that positive energy like a shockwave? I certainly hoped so. All the negativity I had been working so hard to squelch was bubbling up to the surface. I was convinced that the Entity-channeling businessman was an accomplished scam artist, as were his minions. There was no sympathy for us, no extra help for a clearly sick and disabled woman, and certainly with everything we had talked about the night before, no special audience. Even my mom saw my disappointment. She touched my arm and looked me in the eyes and said, "You did your best. I don't care if I am not the only one asking a question. I am just thrilled to be able to go along with whatever program is presented."

I know I should not have been whining and complaining about any of this, since it was a minor miracle that we had even made it to New York. It was so clear that my mom's time was extremely limited, and I wanted her to feel like she got everything out of her time at the Omega Center. She had always made things easy for me, taken care of so much. I felt it was the least I could do for her, yet it seemed like as soon as I tried to make something happen while we were in New York, I was smacked down at every turn.

Regardless of my mom's attempts to soothe me, my heart was pounding. I was so disappointed with how this week had turned out. All the expectations I had were smashed. I wanted the time with my mom to be simpler than it had been. I wanted to revel in this experience with her, but I was trapped in my inability to let go of what I thought it should have been.

We walked around the two current rooms and were facing him sitting on his throne. He was just as out of it as he was before. The braided woman stood to his right. It reminded me of children lining up to take pictures with the mall Santa. The Braid took the hand of the person in front of him, asked their name, and then whispered it to the almost comatose John of God. He made a meager attempt to make eye contact with the pilgrim in front of him as The Braid put that pilgrim's hand in his. When it was our turn, I guided my mom up to him, let her hold his hand, and waited for her to ask her question. I was instructed not to touch my mom when she was holding John of God's hand. I made no attempt to hide my frustration. When my mom didn't say anything, I thought maybe her question was in her head and somehow the Entities would hear it. They would have a little mental conversation and my mom could move on her way.

When she was done, I asked her what her question was, and she said that she didn't ask one. She said being up there and holding his hand was all she needed to do.

My mom decided she wanted to make the most of her last day there and spend through lunch on the grounds. I of course obliged and said I would pick her up when she was done, since I was meeting Tracie.

Tracie was the kind of friend who, no matter what, would show up for the people she loved most. She had known my mom in Los Angeles from years earlier and happened to be the person who introduced Eddy and me. She had been married to Eddy's father and, for a short period of time, was Grandma Tracie to Leo and Julianna. We fell out of touch for a few years, but as life goes, we reconnected again and were better friends than ever. Her mother had died of breast cancer when Tracie was in high school. Sadly, she was not able to have the connection with her mom that I had with mine.

So Tracie and I hit the stores in Rhinebeck. There was just enough for us to see, and I was able to get a sweater, since it was chillier than I had anticipated. I was also able to buy a few more pairs of socks, since I, unlike my mom, had not packed enough. While in the store, I bought my mom a few pairs of socks meant for diabetics. I figure they would be helpful on the plane. It was weird buying them because part of me knew they would never be worn, yet I did it anyhow as if to ward off what was sure to come. It reminded me of when my grandmother was in the hospital on the last day of her life. My mom had bought my grandmother a little jacket she could wear while sitting in bed in the hospital, in case she received any visitors. I thought it was so ridiculous since I knew my grandmother was dying. But it was what my mother did. Perhaps in hope of warding off the inevitable, just like I was doing.

Tracie and I had lunch at a local café to catch up. She was fascinated by what my mom and I were going through and wanted to write my mom a letter saying goodbye. It was an odd request, which she admitted. But she wanted my mom to know how important she was. It was touching, but I knew my mom would never read it unless I read it to her, and I wasn't sure I wanted to do that. There was just too much emotion swirling around.

We talked specifically about how people were behaving during such a traumatic time in my life. Most people were showing up and offering to help out, lend an ear, pick up the kids, or take me out for cocktails. I had become friends with some women I wasn't friends with before and had grown apart from one of my closest friends, who had recently lost her father to cancer. It had been a heartbreaking loss for me when it became clear she did not want to talk to me anymore. She could not get past her own sadness to be there for me. Her father died when I was in Africa with my mother. The irony of the situation was that once she buried her father, she promised me that if I were to ever go through something with one of my parents, she would be my guide. She would tell me everything that would happen and be there for me through my sadness. It seemed that cancer often claimed more than just its immediate victim. Cancer seemed to perpetually leave a wake of collateral damage.

With Tracie, it was a relief to be able to talk to someone who knew me so very well but was removed enough from my situation to offer unbiased comfort. I came away from my time with her feeling better about having lost a close friend in the detritus cancer left surrounding me. It was trite to say that it was a time when I found out who my real friends were, but there it is. The strong ones stuck by, the weak ones fell off. We talked more about how that happened to each of us when we had divorced our husbands. It was an unfortunate reality we had accepted. As we drifted from that conversation to ones a little less heavy, I told Tracie about my mom's cough. She told me we should have it checked before we got on the plane and I said I was already on it. Laurie and I had discussed it the night before, when my mom went to bed. We would bring her to the local hospital for an X-ray to see what was happening inside her lung. Reality was catching up with us, I said, as I hugged Tracie goodbye.

My mom and Laurie waited at the entrance to the Omega Center. My mother had a big smile on her face and was really so happy she had completed her time with John of God. It was astounding how perky she looked. She practically bounced into the car when she proclaimed she wanted me to call the plane and get out of there as soon as possible. It was time to go home, she proclaimed, smacking the back of the headrest.

But before we went any further, I turned and looked her straight in the eye and said the following in as even a tone as I could:

"Mom, before we leave, I want to take you to the hospital for a chest X-ray. Your cough has gotten worse, and I am afraid your lung has filled up again and it will not be safe to fly. So let's go back to the hotel, get everything in the car, and I'll call to see if we can leave early."

She looked at me with a bit of hurt but didn't actually argue. When she heard me say I was afraid, she was actually OK. So I called the pilot and told him our plan. He said that it would be tight trying to find a takeoff time on such short notice, but he would alert the tower to our change of plans. All I had to do was call within the next three hours to let him know what we were going to do. If it worked out, we could leave; otherwise they would be ready for us at 10:00 AM the next morning. That way we'd have time for an early breakfast and the drive back up to Rochester. I figured, worst-case scenario, one more night in Rhinebeck wouldn't be a total disaster.

The sun had gone down with the smell of fall still in the air. It was the kind of evening that would have been perfect to take a slow walk with one of the dogs. When the earth is beginning to settle in for the long winter, there's a palpable peacefulness that allows me to breathe deeply and find a more solid center. It's my favorite time of year.

My regret, however, was that my observation was so fleeting due to the seriousness of our situation. In my head, the likely scenario was that my mom had developed bronchitis and would need antibiotics but would be OK to fly. I did indulge myself in a few worst-case scenarios though. The most severe— fully understanding the extent of my mother's cancer. I imagined looking at the X-rays with the doctor and Laurie only to see large masses of white highlighting the advancement of the cancer growing like weeds in her torso. Being prepared for the worst, I made sure to tell Laurie that if we were to find something along these lines, we would not tell my mother. I wanted to keep my mom in her bubble, since it was where she felt safest. We would fly home and prepare for hospice finally armed with the real information.

It felt like the biggest lie I would ever tell my mother, but weighing the options, I thought it would do no good to bring her into reality. She'd come so far and was still fighting with every ounce of healthy cells she still had. I wasn't going to be the catalyst for her demise.

| CHAPTER TEN |

We made our way down the street to Northern Dutchess Hospital. Once again, I was so grateful for Laurie's presence; I would not have known what to say to the admissions people without breaking down. Even discussing my mother's condition at this point in her life was enough to make me cry. It always seemed that when I put words to it the emotions would flow. It was so much easier to just stick within our circle and try to fix things from the inside of our group. Bringing in any outsiders meant more explanations. More exposing of my emotions. More chances for someone to tell me that my mother was going to die.

Armed with the massive binder containing instructions for my mother's care, Laurie walked up to the nurse in charge and told her why we were there. Grateful we were in a small town, we were helped immediately. We got my mother out of her multiple layers so she could have a proper X-ray, and within minutes she was wheeled down the hall. The only waiting time was for the radiologist to get back from his smoke break.

Laurie and I let my mom rest while we talked outside. We were hopeful all we would be given were some antibiotics and then clearance to fly home. Certainly that would have been the easiest solution for the three of us. The minutes were passing quickly and I was afraid we'd miss our three-hour flight window. We all wanted to get home and decompress.

The doctor came in to examine my mom. Dr. Stein was from Southern California, too, so we had that Jewish Geography discussion of high school, neighborhoods, and the search for someone in common.

The films came in, and as my mother was lightly snoring in her bed, we looked at them together. Initially he said he did not see anything wrong, that we would be OK to fly home. But I noticed something off about the film.

I said, "I see her lung on the right side, but where's her lung on the left?"

Not knowing anything about cancer's insidious effect on the body, I had assumed that it had wiped out more than I had imagined. It was then when he said, "Holy shit—her lung is completely collapsed. She's not going anywhere!"

I am not sure how he overlooked the absence of a vital organ.

Laurie calmly said as if my mom were just some random patient she was coming across in the hospital, "What's the next step? I need to call her GP in Los Angeles and I need to put you on the phone. Can you please talk to him for us?"

I tried not to panic, but my reserves had gotten so low, I couldn't contain myself. How was I going to explain this to my mom, let alone everyone else at home?

"Sure," he said and waited for Laurie to make the call.

I walked with Laurie outside, past my sleeping mother, looking for decent reception. I grabbed her arm and shouted, "What does this mean? How are we going to get back home? None of this is possible. How did she walk around for three days with a collapsed lung? We can't get home, can we?"

My eyes pleaded with hers. I was paralyzed with fear and the understanding that any hope for getting home that night or the next was lost. While Laurie was on the phone with the doctor in Los Angeles, I found Dr. Stein and asked him what our options were. I wanted to have a plan in place before I woke my mom with the bad news. He said he would like to talk to my mom's doctor before he said anything more. So he joined Laurie outside as I sat with my mom watching her sleep peacefully. I was torn. Maybe I could just let her sleep as long as she wanted. I had an uneasy feeling that it was the last time she would be able to have a restful sleep.

It was a good twenty minutes before they both came in and motioned for me to join them in the hallway. Dr. Stein said as plainly as possible, "OK, she can go into surgery tomorrow morning and we can reinflate her lung. It is not an easy process; she will be sedated for most of the time. A tube will be in her chest draining fluid into a bag on the side of the bed. She will be here for a few days but should be OK to fly in a week or so. Is that what you would like to do?"

I could not believe that my late-night lists of what-ifs didn't include this one. It was unimaginable. Was it what *I* wanted to do? No, it wasn't. I had a family at home, two little kids that I missed, and a husband I needed desperately to see. No, I did not want to sit alone in Rhinebeck for a week and watch my dying mother recover from a surgery that would do nothing but prolong her pain. I didn't want to be the only one to shoulder the burden of her illness. I was reaching the limit of what I was capable of doing for my mom and it scared me. This option sounded dreadful in every way imaginable.

"Seriously? There have to be other options. My mom is dying and is supposed to enter hospice care when we get back to L.A. She stopped all treatment about a month ago and my guess is that she wouldn't be interested in another painful procedure. Those thoracenteses were the last of what she wanted to endure. I know she will not be happy in a strange hospital with doctors she doesn't know. Unless we fly our family out here, I can't imagine she will want to do this."

"Well, she cannot fly home. The pressure on the plane will cause her lung to collapse even further into her chest and will most likely smother her heart. She will die, probably on takeoff. However, if you want to spend a few extra days in New York, her lung may reinflate itself. She appears to have defied all odds up to this point, so you could have that as an option."

There wasn't much of a choice. Laurie and I would have to decide what to do. We talked about what we were going to tell my mom and I started to panic. How was I going to get through this one? I had no idea how to take control over this situation and wished someone else were there to make decisions about our next move. Our predicament was out of my hands entirely. I wanted to talk to my mom and have her make a decision so I could just go with that. I would pretend to be fine, if on the off chance she wanted surgery or if she decided to stick it out in New York for a few days and see what happened. When I started to look at what could remotely qualify as the silver lining, I thought I could propose moving camp down to New York City and have our relatives and my mom's high school friends come visit. I was convincing myself that it was a good plan, that this was not the end of our world. I was channeling my best Nancy Barbie mode, convincing myself it would be fantastic if we would have another adventure before we flew home to L.A. Perhaps, I thought, this was for the best. Whatever we decided, I knew I was not ready to face the hospice scheduled to come upon our return.

Walking back into her room to wake her was hard. She was resting more peacefully than she had been in a while. Perhaps it was sheer exhaustion. I gently called out to her and she woke with a start. Laurie and I were alone in the room with her when I started to tell her the prognosis.

"Mom, we're not going to be able to fly home tonight because you have a collapsed lung. It probably happened when you had your last thoracentesis, which would make sense, since it was so painful for you. If you had remained in Los Angeles, it probably would have healed on its own, but the plane ride out here made it worse. It's a miracle you walked around Rhinebeck for three days with one lung."

Her face went from bright, anticipating the good news, to defeated. It was the first time I had seen her face fall like that. Even with everything she had been through, she was always able to pull it back together and continue moving forward, even if it was at a snail's pace. But this time it was different. It was a smack for her, one that made her confront the severity of her situation. Looking at her face morph into one of defeated sadness made me cry.

I said, sniffing back tears, "We have a few options. We can admit you tonight, here, and you can go into surgery to have your lung reinflated. I will stay with you the whole time. It will be a sucky procedure and will keep you immobilized in bed here, for about a week. Or, if you don't want to do any more procedures, we could skip surgery and go to New York City and hang out for a few days, and hope your lung reinflates on its own."

She sat with this information for a few minutes. Her face dropped even more as she digested the limited choices she had. Then, as if she had come up with the ultimate solution, she gripped the sheet and blanket tightly, asking optimistically, "Can we drive home?"

"No way, I am not driving you home, that's crazy!" I blurted out before she could finish, thinking it was absolutely ridiculous, not to mention dangerous.

My mom went back to the deflated face, still gripping the sheets. I knew she would have the surgery if I insisted, but I couldn't. I knew how dire our situation was. The last thing I wanted was for her to be in any more pain. Watching her last thoracentesis was more than enough. No one should ever see their mom in such pain.

So I thought about it. Maybe it wasn't such a bad idea. She and I could stay in our little bubble and hold off death for a little longer. I thought maybe this was something I could control. I was not prepared to think about the possibility that my mom would die on the way home. That was unfathomable. So I shoved it aside and buried it as deep as I could. Sure, she had a collapsed lung, but she had proven that even with her advanced cancer, she could still handle whatever came her way. Her "Screw cancer" mentality was just as strong as ever. She still had reasonable conversations with me, was interested in living, and still wanted to shop. She wasn't slipping into a coma or acting like death was waiting outside our door. She had spirit and drive.

So I went from thinking "Absolutely not" to carefully saying, "Actually, why the hell not?"

I didn't feel like the last few days had been as successful as I had wanted. The visit to the faith healer had been, to me, a bust. Granting my mom this wish to drive home was something

I could do. She loved when I drove, having told Laurie how safe she felt when I was behind the wheel. If I could get her back home, I could turn the trip into the success I wanted it to be.

I was exhausted, but the adrenaline had me almost manic, thinking about the huge fork in our road. I began babbling about how it was easy to drive, convincing myself more than my mom. I already knew she had enough medication, so there really wasn't anything more we needed. In the Land of Wishful Thinking, maybe the extra days would help heal her lung, so when she got back to Los Angeles, hospice could be held off for a bit more. I was using this last trip as insurance that my mom wouldn't die. On the road, I reasoned with myself, I would be in control of everything.

Dr. Stein came back in as we were discussing our plans. Once he heard them he said directly to my mom, "As your doctor, I cannot in good conscience recommend that you leave. You're clearly not well enough to go anywhere. But given these bizarre circumstances, it really would be possible for you to drive home if you avoid any altitude. But you have to understand, you would be going against your doctor's orders."

I was so amped up thinking about our new plan that I completely ignored his last statement. I really didn't know what the ramifications of going against doctor's orders were, but it felt rather liberating. Like I was bucking the system to save my mom from another procedure. Like I was in control. I understood this kind and understanding doctor was covering his bases. Something else, though—he knew how dire our situation was, even though my mom had survived a week with only one functioning lung. I could see in his eyes that he was sympathetic to what I was going through. I was certain, if it was his mom, he would have opted for one last adventure instead of surgery.

"What about a train?" I asked, trying to engage him in our plan.

"They go through the Rockies. I wouldn't recommend that either."

"So, if we drove home and we took the southern route, we could actually do this?"

I didn't know why I wanted his blessing on this; we had already decided we were driving home. I was gearing up for a late night of looking up western routes, figuring out our rest stops, food, and how many miles we had to cover each day. The list of road-trip details grew, and it was the perfect thing to keep my mind off my dying mom. These were concrete details I could readily manage.

"Yes, but don't sightsee. Stay on the major highways and keep track of where the local hospitals are in case you need one. Before you leave here, you have to sign papers saying you disregarded my orders."

Laurie went out to talk to the doctor and to check in with my mom's West Coast medical team. While she was gone, I spoke to my mom in private. I wanted to be thoughtful about what we were doing, to make sure we were covering everything before we headed out in the morning. I wanted to be respectful of Laurie's time and her experience with us. I didn't know what she was thinking about this latest development. My mom and I thought it would be good to relieve Laurie and fly a different nurse out for the drive home. We both felt like it was a lot to ask Laurie. She had already signed up for more than she had asked. I said I would call Bobby and Brian, tell them what we were doing, and see if they wanted to come out and drive with us. I'd touch base with Rita too, just to get everyone on the same page, and talk to her about sending a new nurse to us so we could drive home with professional help. My mom actually sounded excited. Maybe she could cheat death one more time.

Happy with this new plan, I presented it to Laurie when she came back in. She stopped me short when I said we'd fly her home and get someone else.

"What, are you kidding? I signed on for this trip. I am in it 'til the end, no matter what."

Then the tears really started. The absurdity of this entire situation was getting to me. Who does this sort of thing? In my exhaustion, my gratitude gushed out. I grabbed her hands as my eyes filled with tears. "Thank you—you have no idea how much this means. I am so happy you'll be with us. I know this is more than you could have ever imagined, but having you with us on whatever lies ahead makes us both feel so much safer!"

She and I were bonding anyhow. With the possibility of her and me sharing the driving, I could preserve whatever safety bubble I had for myself.

So, at Northern Dutchess Hospital, our newly hatched plan was agreed upon. My mom made it clear that she didn't want to go through another surgery, especially one in Rhinebeck. She didn't want to spend any time in New York City either. She just wanted to go home.

It was time to let my family know what was happening.

I had a feeling I was in for an argument from my family members, since my previous calls to them had been cheerful and optimistic. I had kept everything upbeat so I wouldn't have to explain too much. However, this was going to be different. I had let Bobby know we were going to get a chest X-ray but had downplayed it so I didn't worry him. At this point, I had

so much more information than they did. I had lived with my
mom for the last three days and watched her coughing fits and
talking in her sleep. I now knew death was not far, but I did not
want to do anything to facilitate it. I wanted to be smart about
our plan, but I also knew, based on my mom's wishes, it had
become our only choice.

I slipped out to the car to call Mike. His birthday was on Oc-
tober 3, and with this change of events, I was going to miss it.
When Mike answered with his cheerful voice, I couldn't speak.
I started to sob.

All of the emotions I had worked so hard to shove so far down
came spewing up like a volcano. I just sobbed as I told him the
latest news and that I would miss his birthday. Life had gotten
so messy. I was firm in my resolve but wanted someone else to
come and take over. I had spent the week being the strong one
for my mom and everyone at home. I was shouldering the entire
burden of my mom's failing health and this trip to see the faith
healer and now another medical setback. I had chosen not to be
as transparent as I could have been, because I didn't want anyone
to interrupt our last few days together before hospice. I didn't
want to field calls from my family or my mom's friends, eager to
find out what was going on. I wanted my bubble with my mom
to remain untouched. But now, all hell was breaking loose.

Mike calmed me down and said we could celebrate when I
got home. I cried even more, because I had no idea when that
would really be. I had no idea how long we would be on the
road and really, underneath my bravado, I was petrified my
mom would die on the road. All I could think of was that old
saying that God gives us what we can handle. I knew I could
handle a lot, but I was not sure I wanted to handle my mom
dying in the backseat of our SUV, in the middle of some prairie
state.

He spoke so lovingly to me, reminding me why I had married him. He was the one who could talk me off the ledge every time. He was my even-keeled, fantastic husband who always knew the right words.

I hung up from Mike feeling stronger and prepared to call the rest of the family.

My mom came out of the hospital looking slightly more worn, but triumphant, and Laurie looked like she was not so sure what she had just committed to do. As we got in the car, my mom said she was happy with the plan we had made. She was going home, just on a different path.

Once we got back to the hotel, we made a plan to meet in an hour to have dinner. Back in my room, I called Rita. She'd be the easiest, I thought, since she was usually the least emotional in dire situations. I could also do a little rehearsal with her to make sure my next call, to my brother, went even smoother. But once I laid out what the plan was, Rita just started saying, "No, no, no, you can't drive home, that's crazy!" I should have counted how many times she said it, since it's really all I can remember. When she finished objecting, she said she would talk to a few people to see if driving back was indeed the best option and also offered to call the pilot and fill him in on this unexpected development.

From that conversation I learned one thing: Don't blurt out the plan. I had to give some background as to how we had reached what sounded like a spontaneous and incredibly stupid idea.

Bobby was next. He was rational and would listen without accusing me of being an idiot. It was really hard to make the call because I was so tired. When I told him, he grilled me with questions, wondering why I wasn't fighting for Mom to get surgery. I explained to him the entire week's events, the time watching her nap, the ghost she saw in the photograph. I went on about how I had seen Mom's illness up close like I had not before, and that she was afraid she would die if she went through another surgery. He listened. He knew as well as I did that even though Mom had been ill for more than three years, she hid so much from us, we were always wondering how sick she truly was. She just didn't share her health updates with us, except for a total glossing over of what was going on. We had to speculate, or ask Rita, who was always so protective of my mom's privacy that she never gave us any more information than she thought was necessary.

I plainly said we were driving no matter what. If he wanted to fly out and drive with us, it would be great. If not, we were hitting the road in the morning. I reminded him that the last thing my mom wanted to do was to die alone on an operating table. I also said that if he wanted to come out and try to convince her to have surgery, he could, but I was not going to back him. He was on his own. I asked him to call Brian, since I was so tired I had to rest for a bit before I met my mom for dinner. He agreed, thanking me for taking the trip and for taking on this new idea. He said he was not sure he would have been able to do it.

I had no expectation that I would be accompanied on the drive home. In fact, since I had some time before dinner, I started to map out our ride home. I was set to get up and have breakfast, pack up the rest of our belongings, and head out by nine.

About fifteen minutes later, Bobby called back. To my surprise, he and Brian were both coming on the red-eye and would drive home with me. In the half hour since I had hung up from him, Bobby had gotten on the phone to coordinate an RV so we could ride home "in style," as he put it. He had the entire trip mapped out and was looking forward to an old-school road trip with lots of junk food, like we used to do in college. I cried with happiness that they were flying out for my mom. Having them there would make this trip so much easier.

As much as I didn't want to do it, my next call was to my dad and Carole. I was certain the family gossip hotline had informed them of The Plan. The phone rang once before they both picked up. Before I could say hello, they started in on me with more questions than I could handle. They were talking over each other so much that I didn't know whom to answer first: It was not normal, it was dangerous, it was not well thought out. The list went on. I was so exasperated. As calmly as I could, I cut the conversation short and said I was too tired to discuss this anymore. I was being polite and respectful, hoping if I had a few minutes to recover, I would avoid the fight I knew was brewing. I wanted to be as diplomatic as possible, field questions like a pro, and offer a solid solution. However, I was entirely too tired to be a diplomat. I was set for a fight, simply because I didn't possess the skills to debate this highly emotional predicament without being emotional. I knew what lay ahead. My dad and I had very few blowouts, but when we went at it, it was always a good solid Irish smack down.

I walked around the corner to the restaurant and plopped down in the booth. My mom had the most pleasant smile, like she had swallowed the canary. She was so pleased with herself. Within seconds, before I could tell her that her sons were coming out to be with her, the phone rang again. I excused myself and walked outside of the hotel so I could have some privacy.

Of course it was my dad and Carole. The conversation unfolded, as I knew it would, to suggestions about second opinions with top-rated doctors in New York. Carole had one of them on the phone, and I finally lost it. I had never yelled at Carole before. But I started screaming as loud as I could, just to get out all the tension that had built up over the week. Some of it was not deserved, but I didn't care. I felt I had experienced more in one week than a daughter should. I was doing the best I could, doing my best to hold it together for my mom.

"Don't you think I've gone through all of this already?" I shrieked. "If she goes under anesthesia again, she will die! She's eighty-seven pounds with cancer everywhere and her good lung has fluid in it too. She won't make it. She doesn't want to do any more treatments. She just wants to come home, so that's what I am doing. I am bringing her home! Stop talking to me like I don't know what I am doing. You have NO idea what it has been like this week. It's been one of the hardest weeks of my life, seeing mom's cancer so clearly, so don't tell me you know better than I do!"

I stood on the corner of Mill and Market Street, the main intersection in town, screaming at my dad and Carole. It was an out-of-body experience. My rage was attached to every other emotion that had flowed through me over the last week. I knew Mom was right on this one. The expression on her face in the hospital was now clear. My mom was done. She had done all the fighting she wanted to do. Cancer was going to win this battle, so she was going to take the remaining days of her life on a trip across the country with her three kids. I wasn't going to let anyone get in the way of that.

I was so mad that I hung up on both of them. Even though it was a simple push of a button, I wanted it to be a slam of the phone. Something violent and definitive of the moment. It was entirely unsatisfying, but it would have to do, so I pushed that button with all the force my thumb had. I wanted to hurl my phone into the woods next to the hotel.

Carole called me back within seconds and told me she was just trying to help. I knew this and apologized for getting so mad. My dad was on the phone too, but we did not exchange apologies. If I wanted any help with logistics or renting an RV, Carole said to let her know, that she'd be happy to help. She had some friends in the music business, so she offered to get us a driver and a tour bus. That sounded amazing, but I already had a vision of how this trip would go. My brothers and I would plan it. I didn't want any outsiders on what might be our last road trip. We would be the ones in charge of how things happened. My dad said he would tell the pilot to keep the plane in New York in case we changed our minds or if something happened on the way home. He refrained from apologizing, as did I. I knew that would come in a day or two; we both had to cool off.

Now it was time for my brothers and me to show our mom and our dad just how well they had raised us. We were old enough to take care of everything now without asking for help.

For this final trip, it would just be us.

Together, we would bring Mama home.

III.

ROAD TRIP

CHAPTER ELEVEN

No surprise, it was a terrible night's sleep. I was forcing myself back into emergency mode and, frankly, this role was becoming tiresome. Usually it was one I slipped into with ease, since it kept my mind distracted from whatever emotional pain I was experiencing. Now, in Rhinebeck, just mustering up the strength to motivate out the door was a challenge. I almost regretted championing this turn of events. Knowing it was the right decision for my mother kept me going, but I knew when I saw my brothers I would be fighting again: fighting for her right to choose what to do, fighting for her decision to try to get home before she died. Standing up for my mom in such an unlikely and highly unorthodox situation, quite simply, was wearing me down.

I was relishing the final calm moments in my hotel room, thinking about what lay ahead, when my brothers called to let me know they had landed. Somewhere inside my head, a stopwatch started signaling the beginning of the race to get my mother home. Bobby had chosen to meet at a Friendly's near the car rental return in Poughkeepsie. I smirked, remembering all the times when we had been to the Friendly's near our house in New Jersey when we were kids. I had not been to a Friendly's since we left Jersey in 1977. We loved going there and always felt more sophisticated eating burgers on toast instead of buns. Bobby and I laughed about this for a quick second, deciding that our road trip should begin at a place where we all had fond memories.

My mom, having seemed defeated the night before, was looking quite fresh and excited to see my brothers. It appeared she was looking at this trip with a renewed sense of purpose. She wasn't using her oxygen and refused to sit in her wheelchair. She was using whatever reserves she had left to show my brothers that she was fine, regardless of her lung. The impending doom of her future had been put on hold as the time to see all of her children together drew closer. We were pushing off the inevitable for a few more days with this trip. We suspected we were nearing the end of her life. Regardless, my mother fell into her old and successful ways of ignoring anything negative. She put on the Barbie smile and forged ahead.

My mom sat shotgun, with a firsthand view of what lay ahead. She was more alert and engaged than I had seen her in a few weeks. Getting to Poughkeepsie was very simple, thankfully, since I was most interested in reaching our destination as quickly as possible. My anxiety was increasing with each minute as we headed south on U.S. 9, feeling the clock was ticking. My goal was to have breakfast, discuss a few logistics, and get on the road. I was not really keen on wasting time, since I wanted to put as much space between New York and us as possible. I was also looking forward to Bobby or Brian pitching in on the decision-making. Relief washed over me as we got closer to the car rental return. The week had worn me out with all the emotional valleys I had experienced. Since I had painted a calm and pastoral scene of our week in order to avoid a lot of questions and judgments, I was also a little nervous that my brothers would admonish me for not being entirely truthful about how weak my mom really was. My urge to shield her from anything negative on this trip was stronger than my fear of being slightly dishonest with my brothers.

This trip had been monumental for my mom's peace of mind. She was calmer and more relaxed, even as she faced the uncertainty of the road ahead. I had never dreamed the trip would have this sort of boulder thrown in the way of us getting home, so I figured I would deal with my brothers and what had really happened during our John of God days when I got home. Very little on this trip had gone according to my plans. I would have to once again just go with it and see what happened. It was hard to balance both relief and anxiety. However, as I drove, I saw glimpses of the beauty Nature was providing for us on our final trip together. I was thrilled to think I would most likely never be on this road again. I could leave all of my expectations behind me. Move on to something new. Try to remain open to face what lay ahead.

The first leg of our race was complete. We pulled into the car rental return, and the rest of our team got out of their car and stretched, smiling and sleepy. There they were, my knights in wrinkled clothes. I could tell from their faces, they were ready and willing to share the responsibilities to which we were about to commit. My mom opened the door as I pulled into the spot next to them, barely waiting for me to stop before she jumped out to hug her boys. It was an emotional scene, the three of us there, trying to hold back tears. We laughed a little louder and joked a bit more as we listened to the tale of their trip east, fending off the sadness and fear of what we were about to do. It distracted us for a moment from the real reason we were all together in upstate New York: Our mom was dying. We were out of options.

Neither Bobby nor Brian had slept on the way to New York; they had dark circles under their eyes. I of course was the first to point this out, touching their grizzly faces with affection, like I used to do when we still lived under the same roof. Once we were seated, we got to sharing stories with Laurie about our frequent meals in Friendly's, hoping to draw her into our world a little more. It was clear my brothers already held her in high regard as they engaged her in the things we used to do as kids and how my mom would scold us for being silly. We giggled at the time we had a burping contest at the dinner table. We were hysterically laughing that night and our mom, trying not to laugh with us, pretended to be so appalled that she got up and left us there to finish dinner alone. The relief radiated through my chest. I could feel my muscles relax as the three of us quickly fell back into the way we used to be before spouses, children, and grown-up responsibilities. Maybe this next leg would be a little easier with them along.

Their voices faded away for a moment as I looked around the restaurant. We were the only ones there. It was oddly surreal; everything was so perfectly discordant. Muzak Led Zeppelin's "Stairway to Heaven" was scratching through the aluminum ceiling speakers, making me wonder if it was setting the tone for what was to come. The decor was visually assaulting with the bright lights, pastel plastic seating, and stained wallpaper. The five of us with our various colored sweaters clashing with the decor were perfectly spaced within our booth. I could hear my brothers cracking jokes about their food, Laurie beginning to join in on the fun, and my mom laughing with the same joy she had when she had all her babies to herself. While I could have focused on how idyllic we looked on the outside, I could also smell the dirty water used to clean the floor and could see the water stains on the acoustic tiles above our heads. We were working hard to create the illusion that all was well for our mom and ourselves, while the stage on which we performed was beginning to show its wear.

Then, there was a break in the conversation that lasted a little longer than it should have. I wondered who would be the first to bring up the inevitable. Our silence was broken by Bobby, who launched into one of his statesman-like speeches on How Things Should Be. Normally he pulls no punches and lays it all out so precisely that one would think he took elocution lessons from Abraham Lincoln. His head dropped a little and his eyes looked up with his "you know what I am going to say" smile. "Mom, you know we're here to convince you to go to New York to have this procedure done." His fingers drummed the table, punctuated by his wedding ring hitting it every few seconds. But this time he was different. He was cooked. We all were. Mom had been sick for four years. We knew we were at the end. Did we really have the energy to endure one more procedure? Were we even strong enough to try to persuade her one last time? His voice did not have its usual conviction. This time, he was only doing what my father had instructed, since the argument I had had with my dad the night before was still fresh in my mind. I was not able to hear Bobby speak the words I had heard more than once the night before. Instead, I focused on his ring hitting the table, seeing if I could count the seconds between each clang.

My mom sat there looking at all of us with nothing to say. I thought she was firm in her decision of no more treatment, but now with my brothers there, she wanted to hear their opinions. I was a little surprised, since it went against her modus operandi during her illness. She never wanted to talk to us about her condition or her treatment. She quietly asked if this was what they really wanted. I wasn't sure if she had forgotten why we were even here, or if she was humoring my brothers.

Brian was the one who was most upset by my mom's lack of interest in further intervention. He tried his best to create an appealing New York City scenario. She even looked wistful as Brian enhanced my previous idea of having her girlfriends and relatives come to the city to see her. I tuned him out as well as his words faded into another vaguely recognizable Muzak song.

My brothers had spoken their minds. None of us were sure what to do next.

My mom cleared her throat and with perfect clarity said, "I would like to drive home."

She sat up in her seat, doing her best to take command of the conversation. Her voice got shaky and tears were coming, but her strength was there. "You do realize I could die on the way. I don't want to ask this of you if you are not ready. I could go to the hospital if you *really* want, but I would prefer to have these days with you three. Can you do that for me?"

Seeing her there, making this decision, hit us all at the same time. We were at the end.

She was serious about no more intervention. Bobby and Brian had come there with the understanding that one more procedure could mean the end of her life. Neither of them really wanted to risk her dying on a cold operating table with no one to hold her hand. The time had come for all of us to accept her wishes and to be there for her in whatever capacity she asked.

"Well, Mom," Brian said with a weary smile, looking slightly relieved that last night's plan was still firm, "what have you always wanted to see in the country that you never got to see? Maybe we could take our time and see a few things."

There was no point in showing anything but anticipation for one last trip together. Spending those moments crying about what might happen was just not worth our time. Instead, we threw out suggestions to make this trip a memorable one. Grand Canyon? Chicago? Mississippi River cruise? Mom sat there, now looking drawn, but smiling at our attempts to lighten the conversation.

"I have us mapped out to St. Louis," Bobby interjected, disregarding any ideas we may have had about a pleasure trip. He prefaced his statement with a firm "just in case," as though the whole thing had occurred to him in the car on the way from the airport, but I knew he had been thinking logistics since he committed to the trip. He continued, "Once we make it to St. Louis, we can figure out which way we want to go after that. We could go south and go through Texas or go straight through Kansas. It's boring either way, but we have a few days to figure that out. How does that sound, Mom?"

She was looking off behind Bobby and me. Brian looked at her, trying to see what she was thinking. Something had distracted her, and I had a feeling it was not something from outside. I think somewhere inside her, her own stopwatch went off and she was facing, for the first time, the end of her life. Her expression changed from sadness to resolve. She didn't necessarily look defeated, but she looked like she had come to a decision. About what, I have no idea. But something happened. She put her hand on top of Brian's. After a deep breath, which she held for an impressive amount of time, she let it all out. She straightened up in her seat again and calmly yet insistently repeated, "What if I die on the way?"

We all stared at her. No movement. We didn't know what to say.

It had definitely crossed our minds, but it was not something we wanted to think about. It had occurred to me that she might have been waiting for all of us to be together. Maybe THIS was her secret wish to John of God, for us to be with her when she decided to go. Instead of turning our reunion into something so blatantly morose, I went the way of how we always dealt with difficult situations—with dark humor. We had all been too sad for too long.

"Well," I said, "remember in the movie *Vacation* when the granny dies and they wrap her in black plastic and tie her to the roof? That's what we'll do with you. We'll just keep on going and then get home and put you in your bed. No one will know the difference."

"Or like *Little Miss Sunshine*," she said, not missing a beat. Her body sagged with an exhale large enough to let me know that she was relieved her babies could take care of her in such a state.

Besides not wanting to entertain the notion of my mom actually dying on the way home, I just didn't have the space inside to think about the inevitable. None of us did. Even Laurie looked relieved that we pretended to shake off the fact that her death was around the corner. We just didn't have the energy for one more teary conversation. We stuck to our plan to move west as efficiently as possible. We exchanged a few more details as the check came. One by one we slowly moved out of the restaurant into the bright sun. We all looked up to warm our faces, caught in the heaviness of what we were about to do, when Bobby lightly suggested, before we met the RV in Hackensack, New Jersey, that we stop in Tenafly, where my mom had grown up. She had not been there in decades. The genuine smiles came as we all agreed. We lingered for another second as my mom sandwiched all of our hands between hers, like we were a baseball team about to head out to the field. All for one and one for all.

On the way out to the parking lot, I pulled Bobby by his shirtsleeve to tell him we had one more reality detail to check off before we left—funeral plans. I had visited the cemetery and had the paperwork, but nothing was signed. Discussing this with Mom now was not an option for us. We were going to make those decisions without her knowing, just in case we did end up in that scene from *Vacation*. We were determined to keep the remainder of this trip light and fun for her. It was still too early in L.A. to make the call to Pierce Brothers, so I sent emails home to Rita so she could start that process for us.

When my mother was healthy, she and I used to talk about her death whenever she traveled overseas. That conversation began when my mom, dad, Joanne, and John went to Africa when I was in college. It was a trip of a lifetime for them. Bobby was in college in Connecticut and Brian was still in high school. She had determined if lions, snakes, or warring tribesmen killed them both, I would return home to become a trustee of their estate and Brian's guardian. The picture of her demise changed with the countries she visited, but the details of what would come after were always the same. She would remind me whom to call, where the safe combination was, and who would get certain pieces of jewelry. Being a member of the Neptune Society meant all I had to do was call the number on the card I kept in my wallet. Wherever she was, she would be picked up, cremated, and scattered at sea. The three of us were to determine where and when we would do that. She didn't care; she just wanted to drift for eternity.

She had learned from her mother that it is always best to be prepared. Her mother had made sure, even with what little she had, that every detail of her funeral was addressed, including having paid for an unattractive casket we chose to upgrade. The funeral home she chose knew she was to be buried in Florida next to my grandfather. She was extremely pragmatic when it came to major decisions, so my mom and her brother knew exactly where every piece of silver would go and where her last dollars would be donated. My mom, though, as her healthy days rapidly dwindled, became less forthcoming with those kinds of details. She left it to me to figure out.

One day she had asked me to come over. She had something to discuss with me. I had a feeling it was more talk about dispersing her collections, but it wasn't. She had had a visit from Rabbi Leder, who reminded her of her impact on Los Angeles. Their conversation expanded to cremation, which he was fine with, but he reminded her that if she were scattered at sea, no one would have a place to sit and reflect on her, or come to pay respects. In his insistence that people would need to know where she was, he actually changed her mind. She decided that she wanted to be buried in the little cemetery near her house, so anyone could come and say hi.

Knowing her wishes made our lives easier, because we knew a family who didn't have any plans when the mom died. She passed away in her sleep and left no details about her funeral, or what to do with her possessions. Her children were left not knowing what to do. Did they do their best to figure out what their mom wanted, or did they do what they thought was best? With siblings, it's hard, since everyone has an idea of what would be best for their mom. For them, it caused lots of fighting and tears. I was grateful my mom had laid it all out for me. I would know what to do when the time came.

So into the car we piled, feeling a little lighter that we were embarking on my mom's trip down memory lane, but a little heavier knowing we had a major detail to attend to before we headed west.

∿

Tenafly is a small town in northern New Jersey, about twenty minutes outside of New York City. It is a Norman Rockwellian town surrounded by beautiful houses, mature trees, and well-tended front lawns. It's evident that residents are proud to live in such a lovely town with its clean streets and bustling sidewalks. It's the kind of place where you can raise a family and know your neighbors for many years.

As we exited the parkway, my mom's spirits lifted. Here she was, with her three kids, about to introduce them to her childhood home.

She had lightness in her voice as she craned her neck to find her bearings. Stories poured out of her. She remarked that not much had changed since she had moved away in the 1950s. She said it didn't look like it was trapped in time, more that it was the same, but better. There were more flowers lining people's front paths, a few more traffic lights too. She remarked on how the curbs were the same silver granite and wondered if the neighborhood kids balanced on top of them for as long as they could, just like she had when she was little.

She gave the driver precise directions and guided us toward Lawrence Parkway. She was practically standing in the backseat, holding on to the headrest in front of her for balance. She had a story about every house on the street, including a tale of the next-door neighbor girl, Eileen O'Callaghan. My mom's brother Greg had a huge crush on her when they were little. Bobby offered to knock on the door to find out what happened to her. We heard about the mean lady across the street who was never happy with anything. My mom babysat for the young kids who lived in the yellow house on the corner, making around fifty cents an hour. The parents stayed out late and sometimes she had to walk home in the dark, but she knew she was safe, using the shortcuts through backyards, taking the private time to sneak cigarettes. As we made the right onto Lawrence Parkway, she disclosed a secret her parents never knew. When it snowed, she would get out on her sled and zip down the hill, hoping not to run into any cars on the busy street below.

The car slowed down in front of her house. Finally, we were there. The four of us got out of the car, smiling. Visiting childhood homes was something our dad did once every few years. We always got pictures and reports on his old neighborhood, the old restaurants, and occasional updates on neighbors. But my mom had never cared about looking back, until now.

We stood in front of the house, contemplating knocking on the door so my mom could go inside. She wasn't sure she wanted to see how different things were. Bobby was bold enough, so he walked up and knocked. He was so much like my father, who did just this sort of thing. He talked to the owners of any house we had lived in and caught up on what had happened since we had left. My mom was more interested in preserving whatever memories she still had.

Fortunately for my mom, no one was home. So we stood there, watching her take it all in. I had not seen her that happy in months. She was smiling so much, practically dancing in the street as she pointed out more houses, listing off the names of neighbors long gone. Laurie stood and watched us. I can't imagine what she was thinking, but she was tearing up. She offered to take pictures of us standing there. Brian handed her his video camera and asked her to take a few minutes for us. So my mom, in her little voice, started talking to the video. "Here I am at my old house with my kids!"

Hearing the joy in her voice was all of a sudden too much to bear. I was smiling as hard as I could, but the tears wanted to pour out of me. I wanted to hug her with all my might, but I was afraid I would not let go, thinking about little Nancy and all the things she once did. I knew a lot more stories than my brothers did, because I had talked to my grandmother about what my mom was like when she was young. I knew she was a hell-raiser, but also a good and dutiful daughter, cherished by her father. She was a fantastic and thoughtful friend. She had a great sense of humor; she loved her children and her grandchildren even more. She was also an exemplary humanitarian. All of these qualities were ones I so admired, and they were about to become ideals from the past. All that would be left would be memories. I wasn't ready to move on without her. Those moments in front of 14 Lawrence Parkway would be captured forever, ones we could revisit whenever we wanted, thanks to Brian and his video camera.

Not wanting our experience to end, we pushed my mom for more stories. Bobby asked to see more of the town. So we drove another few minutes to the center of town, where we saw the train station, now a restaurant. It had been where her father took the train into the city for work every day. I asked to see where she had her first job scooping ice cream. She didn't have it for more than a few weeks, though. She gave out too many free scoops and was fired. We passed her elementary school and some of her friends' houses, even the gas station where her first motorcycle-riding boyfriend worked.

It was everything we needed, seeing our mom's childhood laid out before us. It was our free scoop of ice cream from her. We shared her happiness at what we were witnessing.

Brian suggested we drive by our former homes in Emerson and Woodcliff Lake, but we had a major task to complete before the sun went down, and my stopwatch was ticking. Lunchtime approached, and the urgency to place a few hundred miles behind us was increasing. Instead, we headed directly to meet the RV at the Whole Foods in Hackensack. We greeted our father's friend Vance, who then introduced himself to my mom. He had heard about her for years and finally got the chance to meet her. She could not have been more gracious. Vance was a little spooked at how frail she was and insisted on carrying her into the RV to show her what was inside. This was awkward, because my mom was not the sort of lady to allow this. She was independent and certainly did not want to be looked upon as an invalid. Go figure. But Vance carried her up anyhow as we laughed nervously about my mom's discomfort.

I can say it was not a light moment looking in the RV. As we all stood inside, nodding with appreciation for Vance's work, I looked back into the bedroom and thought it might be the last place she would ever see. I had no reason to even think it, but I did. My brothers were distracted with the details on how to operate the RV systems, and Laurie was loading in my mom's medications. They had assigned themselves tasks to keep busy. I was standing hand in hand with my mom trying to convince myself we were only going on vacation. She was tired but was willing to summon up enough energy to look thankful and appreciative for what was being done on her behalf. Vance looked nervous about how we all were acting but went along with it, somehow knowing we were doing our best to keep this time light for my mom. I wanted to sit down to think more about my premonition, but instead of dwelling on the inevitable and entertaining scenarios of how the future would present itself, I focused on what needed to be done before we got on the highway.

We got everything transferred to the RV and went into Whole Foods for lunch. My mother and Brian were looking in the frozen food section for some good ice cream when she said blithely, "Perfect for my last meal," as she grabbed a carton of Häagen-Dazs Vanilla Bean. We sat for a quick lunch together, and Bobby took a picture of my mom with her ice cream. The picture is still the home screen on his phone.

It was evident by her tentative movements and insistence on leaving the four of us alone that Laurie was not sure what to do. I knew it was beyond anything she'd ever witnessed or done. Bobby saw she was having a hard time finding a place to sit, so he gave up his seat for her, shoving me aside to share mine. He was as determined as I was to make her feel a part of our family.

We planned out the rest of our time in this area while we ate. My mom was looking tired and in pain, so Laurie volunteered to stay with her. I would shop for road-trip food, and my brothers would hit the Target next door to outfit the RV. We gave ourselves a half hour to get everything we needed for three days and meet back at the RV.

Normally, food shopping is one of the most reliable ways for me to relax. I love to look at labels, compare prices, look for foods with the lowest sodium, and find chicken stock with no "natural cane juice." This was a Whole Foods mecca, and I had only a half hour to race through for our supplies! I felt like I was on the game show where you have a certain amount of time to fill your cart with things. Breathless with anticipation, I raced the aisles and piled in every item requested along with all the road-trip foods I could think of: dips, chips, cut veggies, protein bars, and anything else we could eat while we were driving.

My brothers met us at the RV with cutlery, sleeping bags, sheets, towels, pillows, blankets, Red Bull, Cokes, Diet Cokes, bowls, plates, toilet paper, paper towels, and cups. I can't say my mom cared very much, since she didn't even pretend to look at what they had gotten. I praised them profusely for their bounty, still attempting to keep things positive.

Finally we were set. All of us made final calls to our spouses, as if we were never going to speak to them again. There was such finality in our actions. We asked for all the grandchildren to be together so we could video-chat with them before we left. All of them were there at my mom's house except for Leo, who was at football practice. I felt terrible that he was not able to see us before we left, because I really didn't know if we would have this opportunity again. My mom told the kids how much she loved them and said goodbye. I had to turn away from the group as my mom touched the screen as if to reach out to them one last time. There was no space for tears. The last call was to my dad to give them our update and time of departure. We had everyone on our itinerary now. Brian loaded up the cabinets, and Laurie made the bed for my mom. We were a good team that day, each of us distracting ourselves with tasks to make this trip a good one for our mother.

Bobby was our captain; I was copilot. Brian was chief navigator with his phone, and Laurie was our reluctant passenger. My mom was wrapped in cashmere, strapped into the captain's chair behind me. She wore a huge grin and had her oxygen on, gripping the armrests for dear life. The adventure was about to begin, and we had no idea where it would take us.

The false serenity in the RV was beginning to fray, though. I chose this time to send an email update to everyone at home, letting all know we were on our way. Now, it had become important for me to share what was happening. I wanted everyone to feel as if they were with us inside the cabin. Maybe if I included others, we could float home securely on their thoughts and prayers. I fantasized about pulling into the driveway to banners, confetti, and lots of cheers from our loved ones. My mom could be carried out, smiling, telling stories of what had happened on the road. My rich fantasy life was warm and safe. I would have liked to stay there, but it was becoming more difficult as my emotions were beginning to ooze through my fingers with every word I typed. I looked behind me, and Laurie was catching up on her emails, keeping a watchful eye over my mom, who was engrossed in conversation with Brian.

Bobby was wrapping up his business day as he took the wheel. His BlackBerry was in one hand and the phone in the other as he was doing his best to keep from swerving. He and I also took the time while everyone was distracted to firm up the remainder of my mom's funeral plans. Rita became our proxy, enabling the funeral home to make any arrangements to transport my mother back home. It also gave us access to the twenty-four-hour hotline, just in case.

We were both happy to have that one last morbid detail crossed off our list, and Bobby went back to fielding calls from his office and answering emails. His confidence that he could do it all at once got slashed in half when we pulled into our first toll and nearly ripped the air-conditioning condenser off the roof of the RV. We looked at each other with wide eyes and giggled the giggle that indicates you've just dodged a huge bullet. It was a final reminder that we all had to stay focused on making as much space possible between New Jersey and us.

CHAPTER TWELVE

Originally, we had been optimistic that five-hour shifts behind the wheel would get us to St. Louis by mid-Friday morning, including gasoline and caffeine replenishment. But things didn't go according to that plan. Brian took command for about three minutes before he declared RV driving was not in his repertoire. With one driver down, Bobby and I were still optimistic we could drive the thousand miles to St. Louis in what Google Maps said could be done in seventeen hours. It seemed manageable, but this was not a vehicle built for speed. Going sixty-five was pushing the limits, since the whole RV would begin to rattle, and taking any potholes was risking a total blowout. In about three hours, we found ourselves hungry and tired in Bloomsburg, Pennsylvania.

Brian consulted his phone for a dinner spot and laughed as it located a Charlie Brown's Steakhouse. He shouted out, "Hey, how about this for fate? Wasn't this a place we went when we lived in New Jersey?"

However, our attempts to relive the safety of our childhood did nothing to protect us from our situation. Nothing in our lives was the same, and this Charlie Brown's was nothing like the one we used to go to on Old Tappan Road in New Jersey. I remember that one being fancy enough that we saved it for "occasions." It was an inexpensive prime rib joint with the biggest salad bar and used to have an appealing dessert menu. This one had harsh lighting that shone directly on our ragged little party. It showed every dark circle and wrinkle. It called us out as frauds, people pretending that it was a perfectly normal Wednesday night.

None of us spoke very much at dinner. My mom morosely reminded us that if this was her last meal, it was indeed a good one. We were too distracted with our thoughts to acknowledge what she was saying. Or more simply, we didn't want the reminder.

Back in the RV, Laurie helped my mom get ready for bed. It was my turn to drive, and I was determined not only to make it out of Pennsylvania that evening but to make it as far into Ohio as possible without stopping. Bobby would take over and we could just keep driving. Maybe I could fall asleep while he was in charge, the motion calming me into a deep sleep. Maybe if we kept moving forward, like my mom always did, death couldn't find us.

My mom was taking her sweet time getting ready. She kept joking about waiting for turndown service and wanted to know if I had gotten a mint for her pillow. First, we laughed. It was a funny comment, and Bobby turned to me with a look and pretended to scold me for not getting a mint for each night we would be on the road. I could only muster a cynical laugh. Was I really hearing a joke from her, or was she also pushing off the inevitable? The three of us urged her to settle in so we could drive, but then she was remarking on the faux wood paneling in the bedroom, how bad it looked and how we really should have upgraded to a better hotel. I rolled my eyes at my brothers, and Brian looked at me with concern that she was not all right.

Of course she wasn't. She was dying.

We had been pulled to the inner circle of her condition, trying to make decisions on what her care should be. We had seen more than our share of fragile moments. Strangely, though, that night in the RV was the first time we had seen her up close. It had been hours of continual time together, so my mom didn't have the chance to kick us out when her facade of happy and healthy began to slip. She was not able to dismiss herself and take a nap, pretending she was too tired to talk to us anymore. There were no doors separating us from the bed. She had to be honest with us about everything, especially with Laurie there. This reality was a little difficult for my brothers. I had been introduced to my mom's true state throughout the week, so they looked to me for some translation of her behavior. I had no answers. Finally, she had brushed her teeth, taken her last meds, and settled in on the couch where she sat with my brothers as I pulled out onto the highway.

Now I could have some time to tune out everything and think about what was ahead. I was indeed relieved that my brothers were with us. I was glad they could have this time with her. If I had been alone with her and Laurie, and my mom had died on the road, I would have felt horrible and guilty. I knew it was something I would have a hard time explaining. I tried to envision what that would have been like but decided it was not something I wanted to experience. As I came out of my reverie, I could see in the rearview mirror my brothers sitting with our withering mother. Over the sounds of the engine, I heard her say to both of them, "Is there anything you want to ask me? Is there anything you need to be made clear? Now is the time. I don't know if I will make it through the night, so I want to know that you two have everything answered. If I die, I want you to have no regrets or have anything unanswered."

Smiling with contentment and relief that they had this time with her, I heard them say that they were just fine. They both told her how much they loved her. They told her that they were so proud of the life she had led. They had no questions. They were just grateful for whatever was left.

They were strong for her, I could tell as they touched her arms and hands, rubbing them lightly, comforting her in what must have been a difficult conversation. They spoke in quiet voices, not wanting the closeness of their talk to be heard by Death. Any tears would have upset her. She wanted to know that we would be OK without her.

Within an hour, she drifted off into one of her restless sleeps, where it seemed she was talking to someone. Her travel guides were getting her ready, as far as I was concerned. It was close to her time. We shared that knowing look that we were relieved we were together for this. It seemed like a real gift she was giving us, sharing these intimate moments together. Our powerhouse of a mother was now a frail, dying woman; she trusted us to take care of the rest.

My mom's mother had done the same thing when it was her time to go.

Shortly before I was married, in 1994, the day my grandmother turned eighty-five, after she had her birthday party with all the relatives and friends, she decided her time was up. She had been living in my old room at my mom's house, since she was no longer well enough to live on her own. She had a failing heart. Mid-morning on the day she died, she told my mom she needed to go to the hospital. Gramma and I were very close; I learned more about her than my mother ever knew. I used to go to lunch with her all the time when she moved out to L.A. after my grandfather died and asked her to tell me stories of when she had grown up on the Panama Canal. Her father was an architect there, and she lived in a railway car that went up the canal as it was built. Our favorite place was Bullock's Westwood for their chicken salad and ice teas, and I would listen to stories about her cruise ship trips from Panama to New York and how she only paid twenty dollars in rent when she lived in New York City.

I knew Gramma had gone into the hospital, but I was at work and figured I would check in with her when I got home. She had been in and out of the hospital so frequently at that time, this could have just been a routine stay. My mom called me around 8:00 PM and told me it was not one of those visits and that I should come. As I was driving from my house in West Hollywood to UCLA that night, Bob Dylan began singing "Knockin' on Heaven's Door" on the radio and I knew I had to get there fast. My mom was there with her brother Greg and Joanne. We sat with Gramma, massaged her feet, held her hands, and told her it was OK to go. Joanne and I went down to the garage for a cigarette. We sat on the black vinyl gurneys, chatting about my grandmother's life, when I declared it was time to go back up. She must have been waiting for us to come back, because as we entered, she was no longer conscious, in the throws of a death rattle. I held her hand, told her to say hi to PopPop, her husband, and she stopped breathing. It was the most peaceful and most intimate moment I had ever had with her, or anyone else for that matter.

It was an extraordinary gift and privilege to be there with her. Death changed for me that night. It was no longer shrouded in the mystery and terror of my childhood when relatives just simply died without explanation; Gramma's death was a simple, peaceful transition from life. Regardless of the fears I had about my own mom throughout her illness, I felt her death would now be like her mom's. I was certain she had taken my hotel conversation with her seriously and I would get my wish to be with her when her life was over. All of this was going through my head as the stars shone above us on our way west through Pennsylvania. Somewhere on I-80, I sensed my mother had finally broken up with Denial and had accepted her fate.

Being the driver was giving me the space to really think about what had come before and what lay ahead. I was looking for any connection between our experiences so I could figure out what would happen next. My mom was going to die no matter how I tried to control the circumstances, but now with the three of us kids together, I was more relaxed, knowing the remainder of our trip would unfold as it would, that we would be OK, together.

Our late-night rest stop that Thursday night was an Akron, Ohio, gas station parking lot. Bobby and I thought we could pull over, refuel, and get back on the road, but we were just too tired. Brian had already fallen asleep in the chair next to my mom. We had logged five and a half hours after dinner. We had a few discussions with Laurie about what we should do, since our mom's raspy cough was preventing her from breathing properly while she slept. It had become her pattern over the last few months since the cancer had invaded her lungs. Before, she could wake herself up and reposition herself. Now, she was no longer waking herself up. We were not sure if we should stay up and turn her over or if we should wait and see if she could do it herself. Her time had to be close, because her breathing had become shallow and irregular. Also, she would not have said goodbye to us the way she did if she planned on waking up and making breakfast in the morning. If we were home, with hospice around, we would have been comfortable letting her slip away. But this was beyond anything we had ever done before.

Bobby pointed out that our mom was always afraid she would drown from the fluid in her lungs. She was petrified of this. Mindful of her fears, our talks deepened, since it was becoming clear that this may indeed be the way she was going to go. We implored Laurie to make decisions for us, but she was not able to do that. She was just as afraid we would blame her down the road for our mom dying. None of us were interested in shifting any blame.

No more intervention, no more fighting. She had given up and was waiting to die.

To say this was a moral dilemma is an understatement. There did not seem to be a right or wrong. The four of us were stuck.

Bobby went to ask the guy behind the desk of the gas station if we could stay the night. Thankfully, he said we could stay as long as we wanted. Brian woke up once we stopped and got up to help Laurie and Bobby move my mother to the bed as her coughing continued. They talked to her tenderly, letting her know what they were doing, not knowing what she could hear. It was quite a moment seeing my brothers, both with bad backs, grunting a little as they gingerly carried my mom. They were so careful, as if they were carrying their own sleeping child to bed. The moment was so dear, so tragic, and so loving. I felt such pride that they were such capable, successful and loving guys, willing to do anything for their mom. We did not want her to be in any discomfort, so my brothers placed her on her side, backed by all the pillows on the bed so she would not roll on her back. We all did our best to sleep.

Our conversation continued at the table about what we should do. What was our moral obligation? Her life was over. Cancer was everywhere. She had chosen to stop all treatment and had accepted she was going to die. We were with her; she had said goodbye to all of us. We had had an amazing day, but it was time. So we let her be.

We listened to her coughing as we settled in for the remainder of the night. There was nothing left for us to do.

⸎

I woke from a dream that someone was sprinkling salt on the roof of our RV. As I floated up from my dream, I interpreted the sound to be salt hitting paper and it had me incredibly annoyed. Why were we covered in paper, and why was someone intentionally salting us? We were not edible. It made no sense. I was floating up slowly when I opened one eye to see it was barely daylight. My lack of sleep apparently was making my dreams search for answers to unlikely scenarios. From my awkward vantage point, I could see that it was not salt being poured on the RV but rain coming down in sheets so white I could not see across the parking lot. Everyone else was still asleep, although I don't know how, since my mother's cough was about to shatter the windows. As I lay there, contemplating another hour of sleep, I listened to the seconds grow between breaths and was not convinced she would wake again.

I lay there next to my sleeping baby brother Brian, reflecting on what had brought us here. What a week it had been. It certainly had not gone according to plan, but then again, nothing ever does. I thought about God and the doubts I had about my own spirituality. My breathing was slow and consistent, opposite of my mom's. Lying there listening to everyone else's breathing was the rhythm I needed to resolve any doubts about what we were doing. No, nothing had worked out the way I had wanted, but what about God? I longed for a peaceful walk in my garden and the sound of the bees pulling pollen from the cucumber vines. If I closed my eyes long enough, maybe I could transport myself to where I knew God always was for me.

But that wasn't possible. Maybe everything had happened just as God had wanted. Clearly this trip was meant to happen. Maybe the miracle cure my mom and I were looking for was really right here with us. I decided I was right about the secret question she had asked John of God. She had her children together; she was safe and loved under the protection of our mobile residence. Nothing bad would happen to her ever again. Her journey was ending. We were meant to be on this road together. All I had to do was keep the faith that if I was able to free-fall into each experience from here on out, I would land on my feet.

It would take more than just a few reflective moments lying there for me to figure out any real meaning to it, though. I was confident this was just the beginning for me, lightening up as my mom's life came to a close.

I gingerly climbed over Brian and down into the passenger seat. I opened my computer, eager to see who had responded to last night's update. Our list had grown to over one hundred people. My emails were being forwarded on to people I had never met, all wanting to send hopeful and love-filled messages to our mother and us. Some were funny cautionary tales about avoiding certain states because of giant spiders or tornadoes. Others were plain hopeful, making plans for when we all got back. I didn't have the heart to email anyone back to tell them what was really happening. I chose instead to close my computer and let everyone think we were still happily rambling down the road. My instinct now was to tighten our circle and keep everyone else out. Whatever time was left was ours exclusively.

One by one the rest of my travel mates arose. Bobby was first. He saw me on the computer and asked to see who had emailed back. He wanted some assurance that we were not alone. He still needed the encouragement from home. I turned my computer around to show him what had come in, when my mom coughed again. She had been silent for longer than she had before. I sat still in my fear that all we had done to protect us from death had been for nothing. But she coughed again.

Bobby looked at me and said, "I thought she was going to die last night. I was afraid to open my eyes and deal with what's next, so I lay there waiting for her to make a sound. I am glad she didn't die but scared she will soon."

"I know," I sighed. "I feel the same way. What should we do now?"

Brian must have been awake listening to us because he said, "Let's run in and get some coffee and wait for Laurie to get up. Then we should figure out which way we're going to get to St. Louis. Do you think we can get there today?"

"Yes," we both said in unison.

"We can make it there by tonight if we get everything we need now and only stop for gas."

So out into the pouring rain we ran.

Once we were in, Bobby and Brian were prepared to get us back on the road.

The night before, Laurie had pulled me aside to tell me that since we didn't know if my mom was going to wake up again, we should get her changed. She suggested we clean her off and put an adult diaper on her in case she had an accident. It would be hell to change her if that was the case. This was all new to me. I quickly shut down any emotions about it and went into my let's-get-prepared mode as we moved to the bedroom to change my mom. I didn't want to let my brothers know what we were doing. I knew that if they saw our mom in such an exposed state, it would upset them. I don't think any man wants to see his mom so vulnerable.

Nancy had on a thick, camel-colored cashmere sweater, a turtleneck, a T-shirt, and her little skinny jeans. Since she had no body fat left, she was constantly cold. Somehow, though, for a woman so tiny, she had actually sweated through everything, leaving little water droplets on top of her cashmere. It was astounding that such a frail body could produce such moisture. Laurie and I undressed her while talking to her the entire time. According to Laurie, it was best if you tell the person, no matter what state they are in, what is going on.

Preparing my mother in this way reminded me of what a former student of mine had done when his father had died. Tariq was Muslim, and according to the tradition of his faith, he was responsible for preparing his father's body for burial. He was fourteen when his dad died of cancer. Listening to the story, I knew it was a beautiful ritual—though seemingly inappropriate for a young boy—but I remembered that and how peaceful it must have been to bathe someone and get him ready for the afterlife. Tariq told me how there were others in attendance, but as his father's only son, it was his responsibility to prepare him for his final prayer before God. He washed his father's hands, face, feet, and arms, up to his elbows. It is called making *wudu*. It was tranquil and methodical, something that has been practiced by millions of Muslims. I envied him and his peaceful moment with his father's body.

While my mother was not dead, I did wish I were in some peaceful hilltop gazebo with flowing drapes and a warm breeze. Buckets of warm water and lavender-scented soap would have been ideal. Instead, I was bouncing along the interstate trying not to fall. Laurie and I were wedging ourselves between the wall and the bed so we could get our work done, but it was nearly impossible. Holding one of my mom's arms while wiping her down made me realize that I should have kept up with Pilates. Some core strength would have benefitted me greatly at that moment. However, it was hard not to laugh while we were doing this, since it was yet another bizarre and unlikely position in which we had found ourselves. The smell of baby wipes filled the cabin in a most unpleasant way.

My mom started to stir when we undressed her completely, so we spoke to her in calming voices—or tried to, given the rumble of the road. Here I was, again, alone with my now silent mother. This really was not the way I wanted the last moments of my mom's life to be. With my grandmother, we were in the hospital in a controlled environment. Here we were, at this point in western Ohio, trying desperately to get my mother set. I could not believe she was comfortable with us wiping her down as she lay naked on top of a Target sleeping bag. On one level, this just wasn't who my mother was, but on another, it absolutely was.

❧

Autumn is the most sacred time for us in the Tribe. The High Holidays are followed by my favorite holiday, Sukkot. It's the celebration of the harvest, in the simplest of terms. As part of the holiday, Jews construct sukkahs in their backyards and eat or even sleep in them. Sukkahs are three-sided temporary structures that farmers used to make when they were tending to the harvest. But when you look a little deeper into reconnecting with the earth and its bounty, it's really the time to connect to what brought you here. It's time for reflecting on your family roots as well as the agricultural ones. It's the holiday that reminds us how temporary we all are and how fragile life really is.

The sukkah is also a symbol of how God protects us from the choices we make in our lives. At the end of the holiday, when we're taking down our sukkah, it's a reminder that everything can be taken away from us at any time. Bouncing down Interstate 71, our RV was our traveling sukkah. I was witnessing firsthand how temporary we all really are. We were living the lessons of the Torah, right then and there. We were responsible for each other like never before, and someone's life was depending on it. The temporary life of Nancy Daly was about to end. The time had come to give thanks for all that had been given to me, since she was the one most responsible for what I had been given and whom I had become.

I took the wheel for the majority of our time driving through Indiana, some of the worst-maintained highways in the nation. I drove as fast as I could through that state, but the high winds kept me well below the speed limit. My poor mother was bouncing all over the place, and there was nothing we could do to secure her. She actually got some space between herself and the mattress when I hit a pothole. Sucking air between our teeth, we all waited for her to bounce right off the bed, but thankfully she never did. It felt like the road to Perdition. Partway through the state, my mother began to stir. She moaned about the agony in her back and tried to stand up. Shocked that she was gaining consciousness, we yelled at her to sit down as I zoomed off the next exit. I pulled off into a nondescript Amoco that happened to overlook a field of extraordinary yellow flowers.

What a perfect spot, almost as if it was intended for us to be there.

On one side of the RV was a car going about its gas station routine, not knowing what was happening in the RV parked to its right. On the other was this tranquil sea of yellow that made all of us stop and marvel. Beyond the yellow were trees exploding with color, more than we had seen in New York. Part of me wanted to run out of the RV, lie down in that field to be surrounded by yellow and the cloudless blue sky above. I wanted to get lost in those trees. The escape I had been fantasizing about was here, was so tangible, yet my responsibilities were sucking me back to my seat. It was like Heaven had opened up to us in the side of the road. The three of us moved back to the bed where my mom was now sitting up. We moved her to the side of the bed so she could see the flowers, hoping the sheer beauty would settle my mom, who was increasingly confused, bordering on distraught.

Laurie stayed in the front as Bobby, Brian, and I sat with Mom. Bobby and Brian were on either side of her, arms around her, talking to her as if they were speaking to a child. "Look, Mom—look at the beautiful flowers. Aren't they pretty?" They were doing their best to distract her from the anxious state she was in. I can only imagine she must have been confused, since she had said goodbye to us the night before, thinking she was going to die, only to end up in pain, bouncing on top of a bed with which she was not familiar. I stood to the side of them, touching her legs, just to let her know we were all there with her. I said I would settle her down, so they each gave her a kiss. They both told her they loved her and left me there. As I sat with her on the edge of the bed, she reached out to touch the faux wood paneling again, this time admiring its beauty.

"I'm glad you woke up again," I said as we sat together, my arm around her, hugging her tightly.

"I love you. Make sure you find my wallet," my mom inexplicably said, causing me to laugh a little at her request.

"OK, Mom, I will find your wallet. I love you too. Thank you for being such a great mom. Make sure to say hi to Gramma and PopPop and anyone else up there. Come back and visit if you can," I said, remembering the conversations I had in my dreams with my grandmother.

"I will," she said with a slightly mischievous look. "I am looking forward to seeing what's on the other side."

I helped her lie down as she started to close her eyes again. I lingered with her for another few minutes, knowing that was the last time we would speak.

The wind was picking up, and I knew it was going to be a tough drive. There I sat, with my hand on her arm, afraid to let go. The time had definitely come for her to go and for me to figure out what to do next. I thought about lying down next to her and letting my brothers think about our next move, but I didn't. My mom was moving towards her death and it was not a place for me to be. She didn't need me to hold her hand and ease her into the afterlife. She was prepared to do that on her own. It was time for us to go our separate ways.

Behind the wheel again, my heart was indeed heavier. It was one thing to think about my mom dying but another to experience it. Inside, I had become rather philosophical about what was happening, most likely because it was easier than breaking down and wailing over what I knew was inevitable. The sadness I knew I would feel might overwhelm me at times, but I was certain that I would be a stronger person because of this experience. I had my mom to thank for that.

Yet I still had held out hopes that we would get to do more than what we'd done. Nothing would have made me happier than to have seen a few more things together. More time, more moments. But the finality of our trip was weighing down on me now.

Once we were back on the road, it was determined that I would call my father to give him an update. We knew we were not going to make it further than St. Louis, so he said he would have the plane meet us there. I told him we would stop in St. Louis, find a place to sleep, and assess the situation in the morning.

My mother's irregular breathing was becoming more so. The shadows were getting longer as we pulled off the road in Effingham, Illinois, in search of showers and dinner. We had planned to shower while we were driving, but the pump wasn't working, so we had to find a place to stop. Brian's phone guided us to a Motel 6, where we took turns showering while the rest of us watched over Mom. It had been an extremely emotional afternoon, and we all needed some kind of cleansing. Like everything else that had happened thus far, our vision of what was inside the motel room was far different from how it looked on the outside. I would have loved to have a warm, clean room with fluffy towels, a safe and comfortable place for me to sit and cry for a few minutes. Instead, it was a dark and depressing room with a bathroom to make you cry. We had been through a lot, and the cold floor and needlelike streams of water coming out of the showerhead were a pure assault to my senses. I would have to save my private mourning time for when I got to my tranquil home. Bobby and Brian took no more than twenty minutes in there, me about half that time. I did not want to be in that place any more than I needed to be. Even the bed didn't look worth sitting on.

We estimated we had about two hours' driving time before we hit St. Louis. There had been a little discussion about staying in an RV park for the night so we wouldn't have to move our mom, but we had yet to find one. None of us were really speaking at this point; we were all tired, drained, and distracted with our own thoughts. The road offered nothing of interest either. If there were any signs of beauty, I missed them completely. I was too focused on getting to St. Louis.

It was a far cry from what I had seen in New York. I drove down hours' worth of plain stretches of nondescript highway that reflected the mood inside the RV. Everything blended together—the gray of the road, the pale yellow of the dying grass, and the light brown of the trees. The leaves were brown and crispy. The glory of fall had skipped over the southern part of this state entirely. Even the twilight was bland. I followed the signs towards St. Louis, quietly singing with the radio, not really paying attention to much of anything.

We were not familiar with this city at all. Brian's directions, we found, were incorrect. My brothers thought we were going to exit close to an RV park, but we soon discovered ourselves in a less than savory part of town. Streetlights were broken, beer bottles littered the gutters, and there was an eerie absence of activity on the street or in the dark row houses that lined the streets. We felt like if we didn't get out of there soon, bullets were going to fly. We were all edgy, each one of us voicing an opinion about how we had gotten so lost on such a threatening block. Laurie even weighed in on directions, telling Bobby in a rushed tone that we should just turn around and go back the way we had come. But we were lost.

Laurie and Brian were shouting out directions with urgency, but none of their directions came quickly enough for Bobby to act.

"Turn right here," Laurie yelled.

Bobby missed the turn, since he was driving a little faster than he should have in the bulky RV, swearing at them to slow down.

"No, go there! I said go right, not straight! Can't you listen?" pleaded Brian.

Tension was building as we became more lost in an area that seemed to get worse and worse. I halfway expected to see fires burning in oil drums and drug deals happening on each corner.

Bobby was cursing everyone and chose to just drive straight. It looked like there was a wide and busy intersection ahead. There, we found a well-lit parking lot of a large shopping complex, where we thought we could stop for a bit and figure out what to do. Laurie felt my mother's death was imminent, since her breathing had slowed down so dramatically. When she did breathe, it was far from the death rattle with which Laurie was familiar and the gentle one I had heard emanating from my grandmother.

My mom's was markedly different. She was fighting the inevitable with everything she had left. It was a heart-wrenching sound, like sobs combined with grunts. It was not a feminine sound by any stretch. It was the sound of someone fighting for her last breath. I envisioned the angel of death standing on her shoulders trying to yank her soul right out of her. After her proclamations about her last meal and questions about dying on the road, we thought she was ready to go. But the sounds we heard were not of someone's soul about to depart for a better place. It sounded like she was having a terrible nightmare and wanted to wake up.

Brian and I sat with her, thinking our presence would ease her transition out of this life. While sitting on either side of her, we began quietly talking about her funeral and memorial. I had my plans and Brian had his. We'd been known to butt heads before, and as our conversation was escalating, my mother's breathing started to become regular, like she wanted to be a part of the conversation..

"Bri, listen to Mom. Her breathing is becoming normal again. Do you think she is going to wake up again?"

"I have no idea. Should we leave her alone? Maybe she had an opinion about her funeral she wanted to share with us?" he said smiling wanly, hoping as much as I did that she would wake up.

All this back and forth of gathering the strength to let her go and wanting her to stay was confusing at best. Brian and I decided to move up to the front and continue talking, hoping a little silence would help her decide which direction she wanted to go.

Laurie and I had talked before about what she had experienced with patients' acts of dying when family had been around. She had shared some stories about the dying waiting until family members walked out of the room before they expired, and those who held on until someone was there with them.

Laurie moved back with her, so she would not be alone. No more than five minutes passed when Laurie came out to say she was gone.

CHAPTER THIRTEEN

I'll never understand what happened that night. I've tried to look at it from every possible angle. I mean, what were the chances of us being circled by men with such violent intentions in that Home Depot parking lot, just as my mother was dying? The threat to our lives was real. We were all terrified.

Was it Cerberus preventing us from following our mother? If my mother was to be lifted by the wings of angels to Heaven, why had there been such malice presented to us as she died?

Perhaps this is a conundrum for the scholars. At the time, I was hoping for a moment like Yeats's "The Lake Isle of Innisfree" or Frost's "The Road Not Taken." Instead we got John Donne's "Death Be Not Proud" as we escaped with our lives, skidding out of that parking lot.

After breaking a few speed limits and ensuring Mom had not fallen off the bed in our hasty exit, we settled into a comfortable pace as we fled East St. Louis and found St. John's Mercy Hospital. We careened off the highway, our collective energies settling down. It was close to 11:00 PM on a Friday night. Roughly forty-five minutes ago, our mom had died.

Not knowing where to park, we pulled into the entrance of the emergency room. Brian and Laurie went in to let them know what had happened. Ten minutes later they returned with some interns carrying a bright orange stretcher to bring my mom inside. They could not have been more respectful, gentle, and kind. I was hoping they would not bump her head or drop her as they took her out, but they were as careful as could be. Her slight frame came in handy; she could not have weighed more than ninety pounds.

Once inside, they hooked her up to an EKG to confirm she was dead. Once they determined there was no sign of life, the brightness of the room became overwhelming. I know they were doing their job. However, it felt so odd looking at a monitor that we already knew would reveal nothing. I finally gave up hope that there would be any sign of life. Finally, my mom's pain was over. Her fight to stay alive was finished. I was marveling at how calm she looked. She was still warm, still had color in her face. I touched her skin lightly, to see how she felt. My grandmother had gotten cold so quickly and looked undeniably dead. Her jaw had fallen open when she died, making her look macabre. My mom didn't look that way though. She had regained serenity through her death. Her face looked passive, beautiful, and calm, as if she were sleeping. Her mouth had formed a beautiful, slim little smile.

The four of us were there with her, waiting for someone to come in and tell us what to do. All the colors we were wearing were more vivid than I had remembered—my blue T-shirt against Brian's olive green one, against Bobby's red polo shirt against Laurie's white. My mother lay there, still wearing her jewelry. Out of all of us, she looked the best. Peace had finally come. There was no more pain, no more coughing, no more worries. She had escaped and hopefully was in a place where she could see the people she was talking to in her dreams.

Our silent reflecting was interrupted by the click of the door as the chaplain entered respectfully. We told her our story from beginning to end, and she was visibly moved, telling us that when it was her time to go, she hoped her children would have the strength to do what we had done. It was a relief to be given such support for our difficult decisions. It was only then that we all knew we had done right by our mother. We knew she would have been proud of us. The chaplain asked if we would like to donate any of mom's organs, but we declined. We figured none of them would be of any use to anyone, since Mom had been on so much medication. Selfishly, we were not interested in doling out parts that would require us to stay in the hospital any longer. We just wanted to go home.

We called Joanne and John, Rita, and my dad and Carole, saving the calls to our spouses for when we had the privacy of our hotel rooms. The reactions were ones of no surprise, just sadness. My father had arranged rooms for us at a nearby hotel, so after midnight, with the RV seemingly on autopilot, we rolled into the fountain-filled entrance, got out all the valuables—including my mother's wallet, which I did not forget—and headed to the check-in desk. I was not sure if I was going to be able to sleep. My synapses were still firing at a sizzling speed, trying to make sense of the last few hours. I would have liked to sit with my brothers to talk about what had happened, but they were too tired and wanted to call their wives. Laurie had made a quick exit as soon as we got our keys. I was still unsettled, wanting to process our night.

I unlocked the door and stood there, uncertain of what I was supposed to do. I had no capacity for tears. Oddly, I wasn't sad. I knew I would be once I could have the space to think about all I had just lost. But I couldn't afford that luxury at that moment. If I started, I was afraid I wouldn't stop. I thought about the number of details that needed addressing—I would have so much planning to do, with my mom's funeral and her memorial. I called Mike and told him about our entire evening, still in disbelief. He assured me that he would meet me at my mom's in the morning and would do anything to help. I hung up feeling better, knowing my husband could hold me up if I collapsed in a puddle of my own tears. I longed for him to be with me right then. I would have given anything to have him hold me until I fell asleep.

Then I called Tim. His first words were, "Oh, thank God she's not suffering anymore." I could only agree. Unfortunately as the months went on, the sadness of her passing would be something that he would never get over. They were like siblings, or even mother and son. The pain he would ultimately feel would take him away from us for good. Seeing us was too much to bear.

I was starting to see how the tightly woven fabric my mother had created was unraveling once I hung up from Tim. My mom was the center of the wheel, with all of us as spokes. With her gone, I was not sure who, or what, would keep us together. My role as communications director for the family was about to end. What would my role be then? Would I have to step in my mom's shoes and be the matriarch? Did anyone even want me in that role? My mom was irreplaceable, but would we all continue together at least in her honor? I wasn't sure. I did know that once the sun came up, nothing would be the same again.

As I stood in my room, that king-size bed became more and more inviting. Its ironed duvet cover called for me to lie down so it could envelop me with warmth and give me the safe place to drift off. I eventually succumbed, not convinced I would sleep at all, since my grief equaled my relief. Was I selfish to be so relieved that I didn't have to worry about phone calls, appointments, and more disappointing, terrifying scans? Would I ever be able to get through a day without shoving my sadness and grief aside? I can't say I had guilt, just questions about the right way to feel. Remembering all the work I had done on myself that week, I let my thoughts drift to more passive ones. She had to be in a better place. Thinking about that, I actually got the first good night's sleep I'd had in weeks. The waiting was finally over.

The next morning, dressed in the last bit of clean white clothing I had and would ever wear again, I lugged my bag down the hall and into the elevator. Someone else got in one floor down, and I wanted to say, "You would not believe what happened to me last night." But I didn't. I stopped in the gift shop to find something for the kids and came across a pen with a tornado on top. A grey tornado with a cow and a house coming out of it. It was a clear interpretation of our last few days. This destructive wind swept through our serene final moments with my mom, leaving us in a very different place from where we had started.

On the flight home, the three of us sat together as Laurie slept in the back. We talked about our mother's life and all its intricacies. I shared with them my conversation with my mom about her funeral and the growing list of people we would invite. My brothers gained the recognition that our responsibilities for the foreseeable future were enormous. We went through the groups our mom was involved with, beginning from when we moved to Los Angeles; the Los Angeles County Museum of Art was just the beginning. There were the United Friends people, the L.A. Opera and L.A. Philharmonic, the Getty House, the official residence of the mayor, which was redone when my mom became First Lady. There were the government officials with whom she had worked to change laws for foster children. Then there were the L.A. Commission on Children's Welfare, the Blue Ribbon Committee, and her former tennis friends. There were the ladies with whom she lunched, three generations of relatives from out of town. We began to get so overwhelmed that we took a break. We knew Rita would have all the answers, having worked with our mom for more than twenty years.

I took the time to craft a final email about our week. It was a difficult one to write, since I wanted to set the right tone. In the end, it was a simple one stating our mom's passing and that we would get back to everyone with details of the funeral and memorial. It had been a memorable week, to say the least. I had always known my brothers were the kind of guys I could count on in a crisis—but this experience together made me feel different about them. We were still in the roles we had been in our whole lives, but now, as adults, we moved past any obstacles blocking us. We were a cohesive unit, caring for our mother.

I took both of their hands as the plane touched down in Los Angeles. I told them how much I loved them and how I could not have done that trip without them. I emphasized how important they were to me and how grateful I was for us being able to get through the last few days with not one argument, not one swear word directed at each other or one opinion taking over another. We had done this together, and I was sure we had made our mother proud.

I don't know about my brothers, but I walked off that plane a different woman. I was more confident. I was less controlling and finally able to let go of my fears and expectations about who I was supposed to be. I was determined to settle into myself and embrace who I was. No more questioning. Maybe it took longer for me to get my miracle cure, but somehow I got it. I was free of what was holding me down. I could finish the tasks surrounding my mom's death so that others, too, would have the chance to say goodbye.

For the next few hours, responses to our email came in from all over the world. We met people for the first time through my emails, family members and people from my mother's past we had not known. I knew how much my mother was loved, but the outpouring of affection and concern was inspiring. I would save them on my computer and read them whenever I became overwhelmed with my grief.

The influx of emails instantly made it hard for us to focus on the task at hand: funeral arrangements.

We went to finalize the wording on my mother's headstone, see the plot we had chosen, and set the time for the funeral. This

nondenominational cemetery was a little gem tucked away behind a movie theater in Westwood, close to where we had grown
up, where quite a few famous people were lying in rest. My
mom's "new residence," as we called it, was shared with Marilyn
Monroe and Jack Lemmon. It had been years since I had been
there. As kids, we used to ride bikes on those paths around the
cemetery; it was a beautiful and intimate spot. I knew my mom
would be happy with the plot we had chosen for her, a little
corner with its own granite bench.

Kathleen greeted us and brought us into the offices to finalize
the plans. We were moving swiftly through the decisions, each
one so carefully posed to us by Kathleen. She remarked that
when it was our time to go, we could all be buried together. My
mom's plot was large enough to accommodate all of us. Both
my brothers nodded in approval, like this was the best idea they
had ever heard of.

I had a different reaction.

I cried. About what, I didn't know. I am sure it was an accumulation of the week's events, but it was more than that.

"That's not what I want!" I yelled, choking back tears. "Before you make a decision about MY eternity, perhaps you
should ask. I don't want to be buried."

Here I was, undoing all the calm we had presented to Kathleen. Now we would become some bunch of crazies arguing
about something that had no relevance to the situation at hand.

They looked at me, shocked.

"OK, that's fine. We don't have to decide this now; we can
wait," said Bobby as he put his hand on my back, trying to get
me to calm down. I knew my face was red and my posture read
as if I was ready for a fight.

I didn't want to be buried, since I was convinced it would
undo everything I had learned about myself. How could I just

go into the ground when the places that made me happiest were the outdoors? I wanted to float for eternity and let the wind settle me where it felt right.

I had learned one thing about myself: I didn't fit in a box. I was a free spirit, interested in taking in as much as I could before I died. I didn't want the restrictions of being conventional. I knew I was far from that. I had no idea who I would be when I died, what my stature would be, but I was certain that if I chose to float on the wind for eternity, everyone who knew me would understand.

I didn't want to be in with everyone else; I wanted to continue to be useful. Maybe fertilize a garden, be fish food. I wanted any available parts to be recycled and the rest turned to ash. Really, I wanted a Viking funeral, where I'd be put out in a boat and set on fire—something really dramatic, mythical, and oddly romantic.

I kept my epiphany to myself, since now was not the time to proclaim how the week had been one of the biggest growth experiences of my life. None of what we were doing at the moment focused on me anyhow. So I calmed down and thanked them for putting our communal burial on hold.

Once we had all that situated, signed, and paid for, we were congratulated on our ability to get through the process so quickly, regardless of my hysterics. We were told that they braced themselves for when siblings came in to bury a parent. It never went smoothly; someone always wanting more control than the others. Usually there were fights and more tears or, even worse, such sadness and inability to cope, the employees had to make all the decisions on their own and hope there would be no changes once the paperwork was signed.

Walking in the door to my mom's house in town meant everything was going to be set in motion. So I took a few deep
breaths first. I had to push all my emotions aside for the next
few weeks, there was so much to get done. Rita and Melida
were there, as was Mike. The first emotional hurdle was my
mom's little Yorkie, Lily, who was frantically running around
looking for my mom. She was inconsolable, as if she knew what
had happened. Eventually, she was going to come home with
me, but for the moment, she was staying with Melida until the
house was cleared out and sold. Calming her was not easy. She
whined and cried for a long time.

One by one, family and Team Nancy and others showed up.

There were more tears than I could handle. No one is ever
really prepared for the death of a loved one, even during a pro-
longed illness. One can argue that their loved one was taken
too soon. Even knowing this, we all knew my mom was close to
death when she left. Again, I fell into the role of steady consoler.
It was such an automatic way for me to act around others and
made me feel better that I could offer comfort to those around
me grieving. I listened to everyone's sadness and regret that they
did not have one more chance to talk to my mom. Interestingly, more than one person said that the last time they saw my
mother, they knew it would be the last.

My next stop on the grieving train was to see the kids at
Eddy's house. My biggest concern was Leo not having had the
chance to say goodbye to her when the other kids were there
for the video chat. Leo had been very close to his Nana. But
as her health declined, he began to pull away. Normally a boy
who used his words better than most adults, Leo was not able
to talk about my mom at all. He was so angry with her for not
taking care of herself when the cancer came back. His sadness

over the possibility of losing her was more than he could voice. I knew he would have the hardest time; it was just too much for my little boy to handle. Her illness prevented her from doing all the fun things they used to do.

When Mike and I got to Eddy's house, the kids were upstairs in their rooms, doing their thing. We all went up together and sat on Leo's floor. I didn't have to say anything, because Julianna's first question was, "Is Nana dead?"

"Yes," I answered, "she is."

Leo was furious. He threw down his toys and grunted the grunt I was so familiar with. He used it for when the words didn't come. It was reserved for the unspeakable. His big green eyes filled with tears so big I could catch them on my fingers. His sadness was deeper than he could express. His relationship with her was deeper than that of the other grandchildren. It was the pure, unconditional, no-holds-barred love between a grandma and a grandchild.

I explained in terms that my two elementary school kids could understand, but they were so much more savvy than that. We had a goldfish once that had died prematurely, as most do. One morning the kids came down to the kitchen and saw Mr. Fish resting on top of the water, eyes cloudy and mouth agape. I could have lied and said he was sleeping and gone out to get a replacement, but instead, when they asked me why he was floating, I said, "Mr. Fish died. It happens; no one knows why. What shall we do with him?"

I gave them a choice of a burial at sea via the toilet, or a backyard funeral. They opted for the full funeral with flowers and everything. So, as far as they were concerned, death happens and there's no two ways about it. Sometimes it comes fast, like with Mr. Fish, or really slow, like with Nana.

Julianna, in her infinite wisdom, said, "Well, maybe she's with her Gramma Euphemia and PopPop and Great Gramma Anita. I bet she feels better up there."

Leo would hold on to his anger for a few years. He just didn't know how to talk about it, and I think he was afraid of his feelings. Once he was calm enough to have a conversation, I promised to take him to her house so he could find things to remember her by. He thought that was OK but wasn't sure he wanted to be there without her. My little guy was such a ball of emotion. I told him that if he was open to it, I would tell Nana stories as often as he wanted to hear them.

Saturday night was a blur as I fell into bed and slept well into the morning. Mike came in, gently laying the newspaper next to me. There on the cover was a ridiculous picture of my mother standing on a staircase holding her Yorkie. It was one I had not seen before, but it did make me laugh. It made her look like someone poised for a grand entrance into some high-society afternoon tea. She looked rather regal, but it really didn't capture who she was. She was so much more than that photo.

We set the funeral for October 10. There was a lot to do with accommodating incoming family, juggling the kids, and trying to keep everything as normal as possible. There were a few people who wanted to see my mom before she was cremated, so I had to arrange for a quick viewing. We weren't going to open it up to anyone other than those closest to the family. So at 11:00 AM on Monday, October 5, Brian's wife Cindy, her mother Lupe, Joanne, John, and Melida showed up to see Nancy one last time. I walked into the little room they had set up for us. My mother was in a small, nondescript box. I remember it being cardboard. She was dressed the same as when I had dressed her in the RV, but her hair was combed to the side.

I am not sure what I had expected. Maybe she would be magically transformed into a body ready for a proper open-casket funeral, somehow dressed in something fancy, as if she were sleeping. But she looked like she had in the hospital. Everyone who came in to see her remarked on her hair. Melida was appalled. She said my mother never would have worn her hair like that, so she pulled a brush out of her purse and styled it in a way my mother would have appreciated. There were very few words, just lots of tears and hugs.

The entire exchange at this point was uncomfortable, but I put up with it, since everyone deserved to have whatever time they needed to say goodbye. Being respectful of how my loved ones dealt with death was extremely important, since I didn't want anyone to feel as if their final moments with my mom were rushed or trivial. I would have stayed there for hours if they wanted to be there, reflecting or praying. I could have been one of the attending funeral home employees, standing graciously, listening to stories and watching tears flow, offering comfort and nodding to acknowledge how deep their loss was. Anything for the people who loved my mom.

But I had my mind on other things.

She was gone. I had my goodbyes in Indiana and St. Louis. Here in Los Angeles, she was just a body, a former home to one of the most extraordinary spirits to ever exist. The urn she was about to fill wouldn't contain anything but her corporeal being. Who she really was had left. She was off, moving on to the next adventure. Maybe she was enjoying foie gras and champagne in Paris or tandoori chicken in India, but I knew she was far away from where I stood. For the first time, after all that had happened, I was ready to move on. Because I knew she had.

October 10 came quickly. Family and friends poured in from back east and Canada. Those invited came, as per instructions on the invitation, in their finest shoes. It was only fitting that we should honor one of the greatest shoe collections in California. It was emotional, concise, and inspirational. We only invited the closest of friends and relatives, saving the larger list for the memorial in a few weeks. A few guests stood to share stories. My brothers and I stood together, taking the opportunity to thank Rita, Tim, and the rest of Team Nancy for helping us through the last four years in the House of Cancer. At the graveside, Brian's son Quinn, who shared my mom's love of sweets, threw candy in the ground near my mom's urn. Something sweet for her voyage.

At her memorial a few weeks later, I concluded my talk with these words:

> Our mom died too soon. Bobby said that she would have been the best old lady, speeding around in her little Mercedes with those big glasses, dressed to the nines, lots of candy for the grandkids, off to lunches with her girlfriends and on to her next project. As Brian said, our mom's energy has shifted and has been dispersed into all of us. Look around and see who came to honor her. Each person here tonight had a unique relationship with my mom, but the experience is the same. She has changed our lives, and we will be better people because of her influence. We have no idea what will transpire after tonight. People who never met may start talking about their personal Nancy experience. But I guarantee, connections will be made, and once again, Nancy would have made it happen.

Yes, it's an enormous loss to all of us. But she left knowing eventually we would be OK without her. She'll continue to be the champion on our shoulder, always there to answer the now famous question: What would Nancy do? Right now, she'd celebrate her ultimate accomplishment: all of us making changes, moving forward together, with the confidence she instilled in each of us.

A year and two days later, I drove down Pacific Coast Highway for one last visit to the beach house. I started to get a nervous stomach and my chest tightened up. In the past, it would have taken a few cigarettes to calm me down, but now music was my medicine. So at the light where Sunset Boulevard meets the Pacific Ocean, I put on some Dave Matthews. I needed something familiar, so I chose the album I listened to the first time I ever pulled into the finished driveway, *Busted Stuff*, and one lyric caught my ear: "Where you go is where I want to be." It was true; wherever my mom went, I wanted to be.

But now I could not follow. I was alone. It was my turn to be the grown-up.

For the next twenty minutes on that cold grey day, I thought about how much had happened in that year while settling her estate and how badly I missed her. I thought about all the conversations I had with her in my dreams, where she told me in each one she now had a chance to start over. One was in the RV. We had made it back to Los Angeles. She wanted to get out at her house and call her friends to tell them she had made it home and she was much better. As she grabbed the handle to exit the door, I said to her, "You can't leave here. You're dead. If you leave, everyone will know this entire trip was a sham. There is no starting over for you here. You have to stay. I can leave and start over, but you're dead. You have to stay."

Another dream had her and me floating, on a huge mattress, down a rapid river. Again, she said how happy she was that she could have a fresh start. I looked at her quizzically and said, "Once we're done here, I am getting off and you're not. You have to continue. I get the fresh start. You have to continue." She looked at me with knowing eyes and said, "Yes, that's right. I am moving on to something new. You're staying. OK. I understand." We rode the rapids together until I slipped off into a calm pool and walked out of the river.

Another dream: I was in a huge house, empty of all furniture, except for rows of Limoges boxes. The elaborate light fixtures were covered in sheets. I knew it was my mother's house, but not one I had ever seen before. She came out on the balcony, holding layers of tissue paper, ready to wrap up the boxes that lined the cavernous room below, where I stood. She wore a long white gown and looked like a ghost. I asked her what had happened to all the furniture. She said, "Everything is gone." She floated down with the tissue paper, wrapping Limoges boxes as she came closer to the floor. "It's time to move on. I have, so you should too." I asked, "What about all the parties? What about the music and dancing?" She took my hand and said, "That was for another time. It was fun, wasn't it? But now it's time to go. I'm leaving shortly, so I will see you again, when the time is right." I said in protest, "But I want to stay with you now. Maybe we can have one more party?"

But she had already left.

I hope she comes back, but I have not seen her in that way again. Maybe she knew I was now ready to be on my own.

I knew, though, that she was in a better place and would not be visiting me anymore. I had finally grieved in the way I knew I would, in private, with lots of tears. Sobbing. And now, writing. The pain left from her absence was excruciating at times, but it got better. Now it was time for all of us to move on, even though her words of wisdom were still so badly needed.

One of those times came when I was just settling back into my routine at the food pantry. I had my community around me; we were in a delightful pace that made all of us happy. Conversations flowed so well, since the core group of people had been together for more than a year. I had come to a perfect balance of involvement that gave me the level of connectedness to my religion and a satisfying sense of spirituality through feeding the homeless.

There was so much I had let go of when I came back from the road trip. I discovered my spiritual connection had always been there, I just had it buried under way too many insecurities about what I thought it was supposed to be. My regular routine of helping others, being in the garden, spending time with the animals at the ranch, writing, being a mom and a wife, were all I really needed to feel closer to God. Mastering Hebrew, or being in temple every Saturday, really had nothing to do with it. The temple only served as the conduit to my community, and I was finally satisfied with that. Taking the lessons from the Torah, practicing Gemilut Hasadim, raising socially responsible children, and celebrating the holidays meaningful to me would be how I would honor my choice to become a Jew. I reminded myself that my conversion was based on finding a faith that fit my personality and my actions. Being the best Jew I could be. Making the commitment to my faith more complicated just wasn't interesting to me anymore. I had no more need to make my life harder. It was time to simplify and enjoy.

Eventually I left the congregation. The more I rose in the ranks of the lay leadership, the less purity of spirit remained. The onset of a capital campaign for our shul took precedence, and those of us who had worked so hard to serve our community fell aside. Though my sadness over losing my community was overwhelming at times, my spirituality never waned. I discovered that I was all right without temple dues and High Holiday sermons. My spiritual place is my garden. If I need an extra boost, I climb the hill to the chicken coop.

God is there in the simplicity of the hens.

All this flowed through my consciousness as I got closer to what had become the spiritual retreat for my mother. The beach house was the last of the material aspects of her estate to be settled. Her house in town sold quickly, which was not a surprise. It was a beautiful house filled with warmth and love that shone through even when she was gone.

But I wasn't sure if I was ready for this final moment. I had been screaming for it; I wanted it all to be done. Now that it was here, though, I was regretting ever wanting to rush through any of it. One thing my mother had been clear about was her desire for her ashes to be scattered on the sea. So a last-minute call to Kathleen, before my mom's cremation, allowed her to set one-third of my mother's ashes for us to scatter when we were ready. They had been sitting in her house in town, at her vanity in her bathroom, where she spent most of her time. I wrote a magazine article about her shoes while sitting at that vanity, with her ashes to the left of my computer. Since that house had sold, the green velvet bag that contained the remainder of my mother had been resting on the living room mantel at the beach, along with Bud, Goldie, and Famous, her dogs that had died years ago. She had always intended to scatter them in the ocean but never got around to it.

Bobby and Brian met me there, to go through some last-minute details, since escrow was closing in two days. Entering the house for the last time was sad. The House of Cancer was now devoid of spirit and warmth. It had become a cavernous cold place. My discomfort kept me from wandering around; I no longer had any interest in being there. It was soon to become someone else's, and I hoped they would be able to enjoy it the way we once had.

Taking a deep breath, I walked into the kitchen with a pint of Häagen-Dazs Dulce de Leche ice cream, hoping to have one last scoop of my mom's favorite with my brothers. A little ice cream toast to Nancy in this grand house that hosted some spectacular parties, and the last great Thanksgiving we had together. I wore my mother's watch and a scarf that still had her scent. I did everything to invoke the spirit of Nancy that day.

We took a few minutes to reminisce about all the Fourth of July barbecues, the holiday parties, the extra-special Thanksgivings. We remembered how my mother had sought refuge there when her rugged emotional and physical landscape became challenging. The kids falling asleep on the bunks, sandy feet and all, the still mornings observing the dolphins quietly breaking through the calm water, walks on the beach with all the dogs, all the sleepovers with our friends or the kids' friends, grandkids skinning knees, sunburns, tar on our feet, late August waves, and the simple joy of catching sand crabs—all memories we would have for the rest of our lives.

As for me, I had taken my last pilgrimage with my mother. I had no more searching to do. No more psychics, no more visits to disappointing faith healers, and no more need for a miracle cure. I could say my final goodbye with no regrets. I would scatter with my mother any residue of regret. I thought about the dreams of my mother and decided it was time for me to have a fresh start, too.

Four containers of ashes. Bobby said on our way down to the beach that it was an auspicious day to scatter ashes because the sky was crying. It was cold, windy, and rainy as we made our way down to the shoreline. The time had come for them to all swirl together. One by one, we emptied ashes into the water, trying hard not to get too wet. Brian was the last to go. As he walked down to the water to cast the ashes into the wind, the ocean surged up and swirled around him, pulling everything we had scattered into the stormy deep.

| ACKNOWLEDGMENTS |

The last week of my mother's life saw more twists than a piece of licorice. In no way could I have ever accomplished anything if it had not been for the people I am about to thank. Even with the meager words I will use to express my gratitude and thanks, not one of them can truly describe how utterly grateful I am for the solidarity and compassion my family and friends had during that last week. To my father and Carole, your love and support has been an inspiration. I love you both so much for every conversation, every phone call on my mom's behalf and for all the cheerleading done on behalf of my book. To my brothers, Bobby and Brian, I can't imagine having done that crazy trip without you two. I am a lucky lady to have such amazing brothers, so whenever you're up for another road trip, I will buy the energy drinks without scowling. Laurie, thanking you will take a lifetime. Thank you for the appropriate giggles at inappropriate times, finding underwear in Walmart, and for not running for the hills when we were in Indiana. I know it was tempting. Nancie Clare, I would not have sat at the computer for endless hours getting this story out if you had not told me it was worth telling. You were at it's inception, that lunch of bad pork belly sandwiches and fries. Thank you for giving me work, for making our former lives on Wilshire sane and for remaining my black hearted friend when I was at my most insecure about writing this story. To Sharlene, my fellow Aquarian, who championed this from the beginning. Every phone call of encouragement got me through my bleakest moments. To Dan Smetanka for making me a better writer, regardless of which editor's hat you wore during the final count down. Every green highlighted track change forced me to dig deeper for emotions and descriptions that had been so buried. It is a better book because of you. To the staff at Counterpoint it was an absolute pleasure working with everyone, you made this process smooth and easy and sometimes funny. Thank you Justin and the Mouth staff for believing in me, fighting for me and for all the promotion you've done. Your constant sunny outlook on everything always makes me look forward to our next conversation. To the beautiful Rita Brown, AKA The Vault, for keeping everyone organized and for being a protective, loving friend and confidante. To Joan Ernish, Pat D'Angelo, Ann Robinson, Susan Diamond and Irene Metzner. Your help filling in the missing pieces of Nancy's early life was invaluable. Your encouragement and belief that this story should be told helped enormously. Maureen Gordon, you provided a key to the past and it was invaluable. To Melida, all the watchful hours toward the end never went unnoticed. We knew Nancy was safe when you were there. To Haydn, Jody, Anthony, Janet and Carol for reading any version I tossed at you, and for all the positive feed-back. To Jacqueline Jeanne, just because you're my best friend and remembered Bullock's chicken salad. Thank you to all my friends who have been excited and cheerful through every step of this book. I appreciate your patience when I was buried under pages and not seen for weeks at a time. Finally, thank you to my husband Mike. Thank you for listening intently to my every idea, whether it was when you woke up, were at work, over dinner, while you were brushing your teeth or when you were trying to go to sleep. Your support of me during this process has been what's gotten me through somewhat unscathed. I cannot imagine a better partner in life than you. Husband, here's to a rosy goat filled future.

Printed in the United States
by Baker & Taylor Publisher Services